SHADOWLANDS

Originally presented at The Theatre Royal, Plymouth, on 5th October, 1989, the play was first presented in London at the Queen's Theatre, on 23rd October, 1989, by Brian Eastman and Armada Productions in association with The Theatre Royal, Plymouth, by arrangement with Stoll Moss Theatres Ltd. The cast was as follows:

C. S. Lewis	Nigel Hawthorne
Major W. H. Lewis ("Warnie")	Geoffrey Toone
Professor Christopher Riley	Philip Anthony
Rev. "Harry" Harrington	Allan Mitchell
Alan Gregg/Doctor	Christopher Brown
Dr Maurice Oakley/	
Waiter in Tea Room/Priest	Geoffrey Drew
Joy Gresham, née Davidman	Jane Lapotaire
Douglas	Ilan Ostrove *or*
	James Holland
Registrar/Nurse	Sheila Ferris
Registrar's Clerk/Waiter in Hotel	Ray Daniels

Directed by Elijah Moshinsky
Designed by Mark Thompson

Shadowlands

A play

William Nicholson

Samuel French – London
New York – Toronto – Hollywood

Rights of Performance by Amateurs are controlled by Samuel French Ltd, 52 Fitzroy Street, London W1P 6JR, and they, or their authorized agents, issue licences to amateurs on payment of a fee. **It is an infringement of the Copyright to give any performance or public reading of the play before the fee has been paid and the licence issued.**

The Royalty Fee indicated below is subject to contract and subject to variation at the sole discretion of Samuel French Ltd.

> Basic fee for each and every
> performance by amateurs   Code M
> in the British Isles

The Professional Rights in this play are controlled by David Higham Associates Ltd, 5-8 Lower John Street, Golden Square, London, W1R 4HA

The publication of this play does not imply that it is necessarily available for performance by amateurs or professionals, either in the British Isles or Overseas. Amateurs and professionals considering a production are strongly advised in their own interests to apply to the appropriate agents for consent before starting rehearsals or booking a theatre or hall.

ISBN 0 573 01894 4

Please see page iv for further copyright information

CHARACTERS

C. S. Lewis, an Oxford don in his fifties; known as "Jack"

Major W. H. Lewis ("Warnie"), Lewis's bachelor brother

Professor Christopher Riley, an Oxford don

Rev. "Harry" Harrington, an Oxford chaplain

Alan Gregg, an Oxford don

Dr Maurice Oakley, an Oxford don

Joy Gresham, née Davidman, an American in her late thirties

Douglas, Joy's eight-year-old son

Registrar

Clerk

Witness

Nurse

Doctor

Waiter in Tea Room

Priest

Waiter in Hotel

The action takes place in Oxford, in the 1950s

ACT I

The stage is divided into two areas, one within the other. The inner area, which takes up most of the stage, is concealed by a translucent screen

Lewis enters, holding a newspaper. He stands before the screen, addressing the audience as if they have come to hear one of his popular talks

Lewis Good-evening. I'm very sorry to have kept you waiting. The subject of my talk tonight is love, in the presence of pain and suffering.

Of course, as a comfortably-situated middle-aged bachelor I must be quite an authority on pain and love, wouldn't you have thought?

Now, by "pain" I don't mean a nagging discomfort in the intestines. For that matter, by "love" I don't mean a nagging discomfort in the intestines, either. The question I will put to you this evening, and will attempt to answer is this: if God loves us, why does He allow us to suffer so much? War. Pestilence. Famine.

He waves his newspaper at the audience

This is this morning's paper. Last night, as I'm sure you know, a Number One bus drove into a column of Young Royal Marine cadets in Chatham, and killed twenty-three of them. They were ten-year-old boys, marching and singing on their way to a boxing match. The road was unlit. The driver didn't see them. A terrible accident. No-one to blame. Except . . .

He points an accusing finger upwards

Now, where was He? Why didn't He stop it? What possible point can there be to such a tragedy. Isn't God supposed to be good? Isn't He supposed to love us?

Now, that's the nub of the matter: love. What do we mean by "love"? I think I'm right in saying that by "love", most of us mean either kindness or being "in love". But when we say "God loves us" I don't think we mean that God is in love with us, do we? Not sitting by the telephone, writing us letters: "I love you madly, God, XXX and hugs". At least I don't think so.

Perhaps we mean a kind God. Kindness is the desire to see others happy. Not happy in this way or that, but just happy. Not so much a Father in heaven as a grandfather in heaven. "I do like to see the young people enjoying themselves." Something like that? "What does it matter as long as it makes them happy?"

What I'm going to say next may come as a bit of a shock. I think that God doesn't necessarily want us to be happy. I think He wants us to be lovable.

Worthy of love. Able to be loved by him. We don't start off by being all that lovable, if we're honest. What makes someone hard to love? Isn't it what is commonly called selfishness? Selfish people are hard to love because so little love comes out of them.

God creates us free, free to be selfish, but he adds a mechanism that will penetrate our selfishness and wakes us up to the presence of others in the world, and that mechanism is called "suffering". To put it another way, pain is God's megaphone to rouse a deaf world. Why must it be pain? Why can't He wake us more gently, with violins or laughter? Because the dream from which we must be awakened is the dream that all is well.

The most dangerous illusion of them all is the illusion that all is well. Self-sufficiency is the enemy of salvation. If you are self-sufficient, you have no need of God. If you have no need of God, you will not seek Him. If you do not seek Him, you will not find Him.

God loves us, so He makes us the gift of suffering. Through suffering, we release our hold on the toys of this world, and know that our true good lies in another world.

We're like blocks of stone, out of which the sculptor carves the forms of men. The blows of His chisel, which hurt us so much, are what make us perfect. The suffering in the world is not the failure of God's love for us; it is that love in action.

For believe me, this world that seems to us so substantial, is no more than the shadowlands. Real life has not begun yet.

Lewis exits. The screen rises to reveal the magnificently-furnished high-table of an Oxford college dining-hall. This is the traditional all-male world to which Lewis belongs

Round the table sit Professor Christopher Riley, Rev. Harry Harrington, Dr Maurice Oakley, Alan Gregg, and Major Warnie Lewis

A ripple of laughter rises from the table. Riley is holding forth

Oakley And all because she was a vegetarian.

Warnie is drinking more than is good for him

Lewis enters and takes his place at the table during the following

Riley I was simply pointing out to her that animals are merciless killers, and regularly eat one another alive. We had a short, and I thought, productive exchange about the moral superiority of herbivores to carnivores, at the end of which I suggested the logic of her position was that she should execute her cats. She then said, "Why are you trying to upset me? You don't even know me."

Gregg, to whom Riley's argument has chiefly been addressed, responds with common-man vigour

Gregg So? What's that supposed to prove?

Lewis I think Christopher means us to conclude that women are different.

Riley Thank you, Jack. Women are different.

Gregg The poor woman was clearly terrified.

Lewis I like her saying, "Why are you upsetting me? You don't even know me." She's right, of course. One does only seek to distress one's friends.

Gregg Different in what way, exactly?

Riley The point is this, Alan. She was unable to distinguish between an intellectual attack and an emotional attack.

Harrington Even so, Christopher, some women are very clever, you know.

Oakley Jack, you don't hold with this, do you? You're a great respecter of women.

Riley Hah! It's all that wealth of personal experience.

Lewis Christopher believes only practising fornicators can teach him sexual morality. Or do you believe each man must fornicate for himself? I've never been quite clear.

Riley In a sense, perhaps I do. Morality presupposes choices. To fornicate or not to fornicate, that is the question. The man who has never fornicated, or wanted to fornicate, or imagined fornicating, has no real moral choice in the matter.

Lewis Ah, Christopher. Beware solipsism. Soon you'll be believing if it hasn't happened to you, it doesn't exist.

Riley I'm sure you're right, Jack. Already I believe if it hasn't happened to me, it doesn't matter.

Harrington Come along now, Jack. We're relying on you to speak up for the weaker sex.

Riley Yes, Jack, why not? You're a writer of fantasies.

Lewis I do talk to women, Christopher.

Riley Really?

Lewis Really.

Riley Name one woman you've spoken to this week.

Lewis I addressed a conference of women on Monday, as it happens.

Riley Ah, but did they address you?

Lewis I get letters. Women write me letters.

Riley Do you write back?

Lewis Of course.

Riley Pen pals. Well, well. Epistolary intimacies. *Liaisons dangereuses.*

Lewis I don't profess any special insights on the subjects. Harry here's the married man.

Harrington Speaking of which . . . (*He rises*)

Lewis Yes, off you go.

Gregg I must be off too.

This leads to a general move to leave the table

Harrington and Gregg exit

Riley is on the point of leaving when Warnie, a little drunk, rises and starts to recite

Warnie   'Twas a morning in November,
As I very well remember
I was walking down the street in drunken pride,
My knees were all a flutter
So I lay down in the gutter,
And a pig came up and lay down by my side.
As I lay there in the gutter
Thinking thoughts I could not utter,
A lady passing by was heard to say:
"You can tell a man who boozes,
By the company he chooses."
And the pig got up and slowly walked away.

Riley and Lewis exchange a glance

Riley Good-night, Lewis Major. Good-night, Lewis Minor.
Lewis Good-night, Christopher.

Riley exits

Come on, big brother.

He knows Warnie is drunk, and he is discreetly protective of him

Both leave the inner set. The screen falls. They put on hats and scarves, and stroll slowly home in front of the screen

Warnie Thanks for the dinner, Jack.
Lewis Decent claret, I thought.
Warnie Very decent.
Lewis Shall we treat ourselves to a cab?
Warnie Oh no. I think I'm up to a toddle.
Lewis Whatever you say, Warnie.

Gregg passes by on his bicycle, heading home

Gregg Good-night.

They wish him good-night

Gregg goes

Warnie That young Gregg. Hasn't quite got it, has he?
Lewis He's all right. Give him time.
Warnie Young people are so serious. Though no more than us, I dare say. Matter of style.
Lewis Christopher used to be serious. I remember him getting quite heated about the abdication.
Warnie Thought the king was unfairly treated, did he?
Lewis No, no. He thought he ought to be guillotined.
Warnie Tell you something I've noticed, Jack. Christopher lives the life of a monk, and talks about nothing but women. Harry's married, and never says a word about his wife.

Lewis What shall we conclude from that, Warnie? That women are more interesting in theory than in practice?

Warnie I find it safer never to conclude anything.

Lewis stands gazing up at the night sky

Lewis Going to be a frost tonight.

Warnie Too many stars. Confuses me.

Lewis Oh, Warnie. You're as bad as Christopher.

Warnie Good dinner. Always is. Good-night, Jack.

Lewis Good-night, Warnie.

Warnie exits

The screen rises to reveal the study at The Kilns, Lewis's home. Lewis enters, and pulls a dressing-gown on over his jacket

Lewis   Here he lies where he longed to be,
              Home is the sailor, home from the sea,
              The hunter home from the hill.

The set is dominated by a giant wardrobe, at the back. It is the size a normal wardrobe would appear to a small child

Lewis goes to his desk, and settles down to writing letters. For a few moments, there is silence

The Lights change to indicate it is now morning

Warnie enters, carrying a tray of breakfast, the morning paper, and the morning post

In what is clearly a familiar procedure, he pauses as he passes Lewis at his desk, and Lewis reaches up and takes the letters from the tray. Warnie then sets down the tray, and pours them both coffee, while Lewis flicks through the letters. He selects an airmail letter to read first. Their conversation now has the appearance of dialogue, but really it is two intersecting monologues; the fruit of the long years they have lived together

Warnie I had the strangest dream last night.

Lewis Another despatch from Mrs Gresham.

Warnie Can't remember any of it.

Lewis The Jewish Communist Christian American.

Warnie You may ask me how I know it was strange, if I've forgotten it. Can't answer that one.

He settles down with his paper. Lewis reads his letter

Lewis She's very persistent. "Which would you rather be, Mr Lewis? The child caught in the magic spell, or the magician casting it."

Warnie No news, of course. Never is any.

Lewis I find that I'm quite curious about her.

Warnie About who?

Lewis Mrs Gresham.

Warnie Why's that?

Lewis Her letters are unusual. She writes as if she knows me already.

Warnie How can she?

Lewis I don't know. I suppose she's read my books.

Warnie I expect it's just the American style. Americans don't understand about inhibitions.

Lewis She's called Joy.

Warnie One can't hold her responsible for that.

Lewis comes upon a surprising section in the letter

Lewis (*showing the letter to Warnie*) Look at that, Warnie. Top line.

Warnie She's coming to England.

Lewis Yes.

Warnie "I'm told you share a house with your brother, Major Lewis." Who can have told her that?

Lewis You remember that American who came and wrote a sort of book about me? She knows him.

Warnie Ah. "I imagine you telling your brother about me, and him saying, 'Is she a nut?', and you weighing this letter in one hand as if to weigh my respectability, and saying, 'I'm not sure.' " (*He gives the letter back*) Is she a nut?

Lewis smiles and weighs the letter in his hand

Lewis I'm not sure.

Warnie She seems to want to meet you.

Lewis Us.

Warnie Politeness.

Lewis A good sign.

Warnie You are curious.

Lewis When you correspond with someone, you do begin to form an impression. You wonder whether the impression is correct. What do you say, Warnie? I see her as rather short and dumpy.

Warnie Spectacles.

Lewis Certainly not a beauty.

Warnie Long pointed nose.

Lewis Leopard-skin coat and red hat. Brown eyes.

Warnie Beady.

Lewis No, I don't think so. More, probing.

Warnie Pushy.

Lewis She suggests tea, in an hotel. That shows some delicacy, I think.

Warnie Tea is safe. An hotel is safe.

Lewis Shall we say yes?

Warnie She might be mad. Remember the one who put an announcement in the papers saying you'd married her?

Lewis Oh, I don't think so. Though she does write poems.

Warnie Then she's barking.

Lewis It is possible.

Warnie I suppose if she's coming all the way from New York to see you . . .

Lewis Good heavens, Warnie, what gives you that idea? No, I'm just a day excursion. Blenheim Palace. Wookey Hole. Tea with the Lewis brothers.
Warnie Tea with you.
Lewis I'm not going alone.
Warnie Well. If you want to, Jack.

They leave the inner set. The screen falls. The downstage area becomes the tea room of an Oxford hotel

Warnie and Lewis look around with some uncertainty

How will we know which one is her?
Lewis I suppose her little boy will be with her.
Warnie What if there are two middle-aged ladies with small boys?
Lewis We must hope they don't all want to have tea with us.

A woman enters, crossing the stage

Lewis Now there's a woman. Good afternoon.
Woman Good afternoon.

She exits

Lewis You see, no little boy.
Warnie What's the boy's name?
Lewis Douglas.
Warnie You won't be too agreeable, will you, Jack?

They sit at a table

Lewis Don't worry, Warnie.
Warnie She'll turn out to be writing a dissertation on your works. She'll ask if she can come and watch you while you create. She'll say, "I'll sit in a corner and you'll never know I'm there." She'll take flash photographs and ask you how you get your ideas.
Lewis It's only tea. An hour or so of polite conversation. Then we go home, and everything goes on just the way it always has.

An eight-year-old boy enters, and looks around. He carries a book. This is Douglas

Warnie There's a small boy. With a woman.

A sensible-looking woman follows the boy, and looks round the room. She looks neither mad, nor obviously American. In fact, she is rather attractive. This is Joy

Lewis It's her, Warnie.
Warnie Surely not?
Lewis I think so.

Joy sees them, and crosses the room to them. They rise. She holds out her hand

Joy Mr Lewis?
Lewis Mrs Gresham?

Joy I'm Joy Gresham.
Lewis How do you do. This is my brother, Major Lewis.
Joy Major Lewis. And this is Douglas.

Douglas is standing staring at Lewis

Lewis Hallo, Douglas.
Douglas Is that him?
Joy That's him.
Douglas It doesn't look like him.

This produces a general laugh

Lewis I'm sorry, Douglas. I can only say, yours is a common reaction. Please sit down, Mrs Gresham, and we'll summon up some tea. That is, if you drink tea.
Joy Of course. This is England.

Warnie rings the bell for the Waiter, as Joy and Douglas sit. Joy is staring at Lewis rather as Douglas did

Lewis I get the feeling you share Douglas's opinion. I don't look like him.
Joy Oh, I'm sorry. It's just that I've imagined this moment.
Lewis And it's not as you imagined?
Joy Not exactly.

The Waiter comes

Warnie Tea for three, please.

The Waiter goes. During the following he brings a tray of tea and then exits again

Joy It's kind of you to find time to meet me. So many people must write you. You can't be forever having tea with strange women.
Lewis Not completely strange. I've enjoyed our correspondence.
Joy Enjoyed? OK.
Lewis Not the word you would use?
Joy Your letters have been the most important thing in my life. But let's pretend I didn't say that. This is tea. This is England.
Lewis So—how long have you been in the country?
Joy Just over a week.
Lewis And what brings you to England?
Joy Oh, various things. I've wanted to come for some time.
Warnie So how do you find England, Mrs Gresham?
Joy Quiet. Extremely quiet. I would go so far as to say, too quiet. The big mystery about the English is, where are they all? And why are they all so tired? Seriously. They don't talk. They don't move. All day they're timid and lethargic. What's going on?
Lewis Do you have an explanation?
Joy I have a theory. My theory goes like this. The English are nocturnal creatures. They do their living at night. Somewhere in England there's this terrific party going on, all through the night, with everyone yelling and stomping and having one hell of a time. So all day, they're sleeping it off.

Lewis If only it were true. I'm afraid we don't have the famous energy of New York.

Joy You can keep New York.

Warnie You're a New Yorker, are you, Mrs Gresham?

Joy Not any more.

Warnie What does your husband do?

Joy Bill? Bill's a writer. Or he would be, if he ever wrote.

Warnie And you too, Jack tells me.

Joy All in the past. You call him Jack?

Lewis From when I was four years old. I never liked the name Clive.

Joy I wouldn't have thought of you as a Jack. But now that you say it, yes, you do look like a Jack.

Lewis What does a Jack look like?

Joy Not at all spiritual.

Lewis Now I've disappointed you.

Joy No. You're just becoming real, that's all.

Douglas Mom? Will he write in my book?

Joy We'll have to ask him, won't we? Douglas has brought one of his Narnia books.

Lewis One of the Narnia books, have you really? Which one?

Douglas gives Lewis his book

The Magician's Nephew. Very good. (*He takes out a pen and writes on the fly-leaf*)

Douglas It's not true, is it?

Lewis That depends what you mean by true. It's a story.

Douglas Digory put on the magic ring, and it magicked him into this palace, where there was this beautiful queen, except she was really a witch, and he found a magic apple, and he brought it back for his mother, and she was very sick, and she got well again.

Lewis That sounds like a fair synopsis.

Douglas But it isn't true.

Lewis It's true in the story.

Douglas Can you do magic?

Lewis No. I'm afraid not.

He gives Douglas back his book. Douglas reads what he has written

Douglas Mom, can I leave the table?

Joy Is it all right if he runs about?

Lewis Er—I don't see why not.

Joy Don't go too far, darling.

Douglas exits

Joy All this "It isn't true" is his way of saying "I want it to be true". I was just like that at his age. I remember actually announcing to my parents that I had become an atheist.

Lewis You mean you secretly wanted to believe in God?

Joy In something, at least. But I didn't know that then.

Lewis If I remember correctly, you've been through several phases. You were born a Jew, then you became a Communist, and then you were converted to Christianity.

Joy You remember correctly.

Lewis But you started with atheism?

Joy No, I started with materialism. I had it all worked out by high school. Men are only apes. Life is only an electro-chemical reaction. Mind is only a set of conditioned reflexes. The universe is only matter. Matter is only energy. I forget what I said energy was only.

Warnie Extraordinary.

Joy Oh, that was all a front. Somewhere deep inside there was somebody else. Somebody lost in dreams.

Lewis The one who wrote the poems.

Joy I guess so.

Warnie Ah? You're a poet, Mrs Gresham?

Joy Major Lewis, I know what you're thinking. You're thinking, God save us, she's going to start reciting.

Warnie I hope I'm not so bad-mannered.

Joy No poetry at tea-time. I know my manners, too. But just to redeem myself a little, I must tell you that I did once win a national poetry award, which I shared with Robert Frost. You have heard of Robert Frost?

Warnie Yes. Absolutely.

Joy But that's all in the past now.

Lewis Why is that?

Joy Let's say, I've turned away from the mirror.

Lewis is intrigued

Lewis The mirror? Do you mean the reflection of yourself, or the reflection of the world?

Joy The one being vanity, which is bad, the other being art, which is good?

Lewis Possibly.

Joy I don't make that distinction. See yourself in the mirror, you're separate from yourself. See the world in the mirror, you're separate from the world. I don't want that separation any more.

Lewis I think I would argue that art has quite the opposite effect. Great art breaks through that separateness, to let us touch the very heart of reality.

Joy Breaks through? That sounds as if art does all the work. I'd say we have to do the breaking through ourselves. Art teaches us how to know it when we see it, but art isn't it.

Lewis Oh, I see. Art is some sort of instruction manual for life, is it?

Joy Hey! That's one of your favourite tricks, isn't it? Redescribe your opponent's argument with a dismissive image, and you think you've dismissed the argument.

Lewis is taken aback by her vigorous riposte, but he bows to the truth in her criticism

Lewis I stand corrected.

Douglas enters, near the tea table, and stares at the bell that summons the Waiter, obviously wanting to ring it

Joy I really shouldn't take up any more of your time.

All rise

Lewis It's extremely kind of you to come all this way. Warnie, I really should settle up.

Douglas reaches for the bell

Douglas Mom! Can I ring the bell?
Joy No.

Warnie rings the bell

Lewis So how long are you planning to be in England?
Joy To the end of December.
Lewis And do you expect to be in Oxford again?
Joy I don't know. I could be.
Lewis What do you say, Warnie? Could we rise to a pot of home-brewed tea?
Warnie I think we can manage that.
Lewis Given adequate warning, of course.
Joy Thank you. I'd like that.
Lewis Well, I'd better see what the damage is.

The Waiter enters

Lewis goes to him to pay the bill

Joy Major Lewis, I must rely on you to tell me if I take up too much of your brother's time.
Warnie I'm sure you have time pressures of your own, Mrs Gresham.
Joy Oh, sure. Some.

Warnie and Joy make their way to the exit

Your brother has given me so much. Through his writing, I mean. I think it might surprise you to know just how much.
Warnie Mrs Gresham, everything surprises me.

Warnie and Joy exit. The Waiter clears the tea tray

Lewis is about to follow, when he sees Douglas, who is still hanging round the bell

Lewis Do you remember the bell in the book?
Douglas Yes. And the queen was sitting in a stone chair, and she was very beautiful, and she didn't move or even breathe. But she wasn't dead.
Lewis No. She was waiting.
Douglas Waiting for someone to ring the bell.
Lewis Do you remember the writing on the pillar beneath the bell? "Make your choice, adventurous stranger. Strike the bell, and bide the danger."

Music begins: the music of the magic world

Douglas Can I?
Lewis It'll break the spell. It'll wake the queen.
Douglas I don't care.
Lewis All right, then.

Douglas rings the bell

The Lights change. The screen rises. The doors of the giant wardrobe slowly open, to reveal a magical infinite space beyond: a child's vision of paradise. Douglas walks towards the opening wardrobe doors, as if hypnotized. Lewis watches

> *Douglas enters the magic world, and the great door closes behind him*

The music fades. The brief glimpse of another world is over. The Lights change again. The set is once more the study at The Kilns

> *Warnie enters, carrying Christmas paper chains*

Lewis joins him, and together they hang the paper chains

Lewis It's only a cup of tea. She won't stay long.
Warnie I didn't say a word.

They work in silence for a few moments

Lewis At least one can talk to her.
Warnie Listen to her.
Lewis You think she's going to make a nuisance of herself, don't you?
Warnie I'm sure you know what you're doing, Jack.
Lewis She sails back to New York at the end of the month. One can be so much more friendly to people who can't stay long.
Warnie What about the boy? What did you write in his book, by the way?
Lewis "The magic never ends."
Warnie You don't think that's over-stating things a little?
Lewis He's only a child.
Warnie He'll ask for his money back later.
Lewis You know what she said about Douglas, how "It isn't true" is his way of saying "I want it to be true"? I thought that was perceptive.
Warnie I wonder what her husband thinks of her running round England like this.
Lewis This isn't the Middle Ages, Warnie.
Warnie She is American, of course.
Lewis And a poet.
Warnie She'll make you listen to one of her poems. I bet you ten shillings to sixpence. Then she'll say to you, "How do you like it, Mr Lewis?" And you'll be stumped.
Lewis I shall say, "Only you could have written that."
Warnie "A distinctive voice."

The doorbell rings

Lewis Absolutely. There they are.

Warnie Is it a three-line whip?
Lewis Not at all.

Lewis exits, and can be heard greeting Joy and Douglas off stage

Warnie finishes the decorations

(*Off*) You found us. Welcome.

Joy (*off*) Hallo! Take your coat off, Douglas.

Joy enters and looks round, openly curious

Hallo. Oh, isn't that pretty.

Douglas, following her, goes straight to a bookcase, and starts taking out books. Lewis, too, enters

Warnie Mrs Gresham, if you'll excuse me. I'm going to leave Jack to entertain you.
Joy Oh. Good to see you again, Major Lewis. (*To Lewis*) Do you mind Douglas looking at your books?
Lewis That's what books are for.
Warnie Jack is particularly hoping you'll introduce him to your poetry.

Warnie gives Lewis a private meaning look, and exits

Joy Are you?
Lewis I'd be interested to know what you write.
Joy Wrote. All in the past. (*She takes off her hat and coat and gloves, and walks round the room examining it in more detail*)

Douglas has curled up in a corner with a book

How long have you and your brother lived here?
Lewis Would you believe, for over twenty years.
Joy Good heavens! No wonder it's so comfortable.
Lewis My friends call it the Midden. They say if I move the bookcases, the walls will fall down. Make yourself at home, and I'll see if I can summon up some tea.

Lewis exits to get the tea

Joy goes to his desk, to examine the books piled there

Joy What have you got there?
Douglas *The Lion, the Witch and the Wardrobe.*
Joy The best. Be careful with that. It's probably Mr Lewis's first copy.

Lewis enters with a tray of tea

Lewis As you see, I'm all prepared.
Joy Sir Philip Sidney. Sir Thomas Wyatt. You like your poets to have titles.
Lewis I'm working on English Literature in the Sixteenth Century, Excluding Drama. For OHEL.
Joy Oh hell?

Lewis The Oxford History of English Literature.

Joy Sixteenth century. You got the easy one.

Lewis You think so?

Joy Well, who is there? Spenser. If you cheat, you can squeeze Shakespeare in at the end.

Lewis Excluding drama.

Joy *Venus and Adonis? The Rape of Lucrece?* They must be fifteen-ninety-something.

Lewis You're quite right.

Joy Of course, you do have Knox's *The First Blast of the Trumpet Against the Monstrous Regiment of Women.* That is what I call one hell of a title.

Lewis Do you really? What did you call your book of poems?

Joy *Letters to a Comrade. (She mimes an exaggerated yawn)*

Lewis Do you remember any of them?

Joy Oh, you don't want to hear——

Lewis No, no. Come on.

Joy OK, let's get it over with. Let's see. Here's one I wrote when I was twenty-two. Spanish Civil War. It's called "Snow in Madrid." *(She recites, a little self-consciously, watching his reaction as she does so)*

> Softly, so casual,
> Lovely, so light, so light.
> The cruel sky lets fall
> Something one does not fight.
>
> Men before perishing
> See with unwounded eye
> For once, a gentle thing
> Fall from the sky.

Lewis says nothing. It is not what he expected

Embarrassed, huh? Well, buddy, you asked for it, you get out of it.

Lewis No. I'm touched.

Joy Touched? OK, that'll do. That's about its level. When was I ever in Madrid? The answer is, never.

Lewis Personal experience isn't everything.

Joy You don't think so?

Lewis I've never been to Madrid, but I know it's there.

Joy How about Narnia? Ever been there?

Lewis Interesting question. I'm not sure. I suppose I've sent surrogates of myself there. Children.

Joy Yourself as a child.

Lewis Something like that.

Joy It is different when you feel something for yourself. And it's a lot different when it hurts.

Lewis Just because something hurts, it doesn't make it more true. Or even more significant.

Joy No. I guess not.

Lewis Douglas. There's some orange squash and some fruit cake, if you want it.

Douglas takes the glass of squash and the cake

Lewis I'm not saying pain is purposeless, or even neutral. Not at all. But to find meaning in pain, there has to be something else. Pain is a tool. If you like, pain is God's mega——

Joy God's megaphone to rouse a deaf world.

Lewis How embarrassing. You know my writing too well.

Joy I know it because I've read it and re-read it. I knew you pretty well before we met.

Lewis Ah, but you had not had the Personal Experience.

Joy Mr Lewis—Listen, I can't go on calling you Mr Lewis, it makes me feel like a child. Can I call you Jack?

Lewis Of course you can.

Joy Jack. I'm Joy.

She shakes his hand

Lewis Joy. Good. Well, that's that.

Joy So—Jack. Have you ever been really hurt?

Lewis You don't give up, do you?

Joy I'm sorry. I withdraw the question. What do you do for Christmas?

Lewis Oh, much as last year. Roast turkey, Christmas pud, far too much to drink. How about you?

Joy We haven't decided. Some lucky English hotel. That should be a new experience.

Lewis Then home for the New Year.

Joy Home. Yes.

This thought quietens Joy. There follows a short silence

Lewis I have been really hurt, you know. The first time is always the worst. That was when my mother died.

Joy How old were you?

Lewis Eight.

Joy Old enough to hurt.

Lewis Oh yes. It was the end of my world. I remember my father in tears. Voices all over the house. Doors shutting and opening. It was a big house, all long empty corridors. I remember, I had the toothache. I wanted my mother to come to me. I cried for her to come, but she didn't come.

Joy What was it?

Lewis It was cancer. It followed the usual course. An operation. An apparent recovery. A return of the disease. Increasing pain. Death.

Joy And after death? Did you believe in heaven, when you were a child? Did you believe you'd see her again?

Lewis No. She was gone. That was all.

Joy And you went somewhere secret to cry?

Lewis I went somewhere secret. I didn't cry.

They both fall silent again. Joy, feeling she has come close to him, is about to continue at this more personal level, when he turns away

Douglas. There's some more orange squash, if you'd like.

Joy No thanks, Jack. We should go.

Lewis Oh? So soon? You only just got here. Well, I'm very glad you came.

Joy I'm very glad you asked me. (*She rises*) Douglas. Book back. Coat on.

Douglas does as he is told

Lewis He doesn't make a fuss, does he?

Joy Douglas and I understand each other.

Lewis Joy, I don't like to think of you Christmassing in an hotel. Why don't you both come here? You'd be very welcome.

Joy No, no. You don't want strangers rampaging all over your house.

Lewis I'll have to ask Warnie, of course. But speaking for myself, I would welcome the company.

Joy (*as she goes*) It's very kind of you, Jack. You ask Warnie. But we can look after ourselves, I promise you. We're very independent, aren't we, Douglas?

Douglas Yup.

Joy and Douglas exit

Lewis (*following them*) You'd be doing me a kindness. I'm sure Warnie will be delighted.

Lewis exits

Warnie, Riley, Oakley and Harrington enter, all carrying glasses, singing a carol. This is a pre-Christmas drinks party

Riley gazes at the Christmas decorations

Lewis enters

All   In dulci jubilo
                                Now sing with hearts aglow!
                                Our delight and pleasure
                                Lies in praesepio,
                                Like sunshine is our treasure
                                Matris in gremio.
                                Alpha es et O!

Lewis Thank you, Maurice. Well done.

Riley What I resent about Christmas is the general presumption of good will. I feel no good will towards my fellow men. I feel ill will.

Lewis It's got nothing to do with how you feel, Christopher. Feelings are far too unreliable.

Riley Maybe so, Jack, but they're very close to me. I'm very attached to my feelings. I won't hear a word against them. They're easily hurt.

Harrington I'm afraid Christmas is something of a lost cause, Jack.

Lewis That depends on how it's presented. If you tell people it's about peace in the world, and being kind to the poor and needy, then naturally nobody listens.

Riley Aha, the arch communicator in action. Give us the sales pitch, Jack.

Lewis Virgin Has Sex With Omnipotent Alien. Gives Birth to God.

Riley I've always thought the incarnation proves that God has a severely limited intellect. Who'd choose, voluntarily, to be human, when you have the option of staying safely divine?

Lewis Think of the magic, Christopher. The birth of a helpless squealing creature who is also God. An all-powerful baby. Doesn't that satisfy your taste for the peculiar? It's the coming of new life in the heart of winter, when all the land is dead. The snow falls, and the trees are bare. All but one tree, which bears fruit. That's real magic.

Harrington I think you're a little hard on the poor and needy, Jack. No room at the inn, remember?

Warnie Jack's invited them to stay with us.

Riley Really, Jack?

Harrington Who?

Warnie Mother and child. They're upstairs.

Lewis Mrs Gresham and her son. They're spending Christmas with us.

Riley Well, Jack, you have succeeded in surprising me. Who is Mrs Gresham?

Lewis Wait and see.

Warnie She's an American.

Riley Curiouser and curiouser.

Joy enters

Joy Merry Christmas!

Lewis Ah, Joy. Let me introduce you. Dr Maurice Oakley. The Reverend Harry Harrington. Professor Christopher Riley. Mrs Joy Gresham.

Harrington Delighted to meet you, Mrs Gresham.

Riley Mrs Gresham, how opportune. I understand you're from the United States of America.

Joy Yes, I am.

Riley Then perhaps you can satisfy my curiosity on a small matter. Jack's children's stories are published in America, they tell me. Are they or are they not in translation?

Joy I don't understand.

Riley "The Lion, the Witch, and the Clothes-Closet"?

Lewis Behave yourself, Christopher.

Riley Forgive me, Jack. Success breeds envy, as ever.

Lewis I don't know what you call success. Most of my friends treat my children's books as a form of juvenile dementia.

Joy Have you read any of them, Professor Riley?

Riley Jack has read extracts aloud to me. It is one of his tests of friendship.

Joy He's been reading me Sir Philip Sidney.

Riley Is that more bearable?

Joy Bearable? Sidney's glorious.

Her unselfconscious enthusiasm clearly delights Lewis

Lewis He is, isn't he?

Joy He has this inspired image of Desire, capital D, as a baby that won't stop
bawling. "Sleep, baby mine, Desire, Nurse Beauty singeth"——

Lewis "Thy cries, O baby, set mine head on aching." I'm afraid Sidney was
rather down on desire.

Joy Babies just yell until they get what they want. That's what I love about
the image. It's precise. Nowadays, poets are so lazy.

Lewis You sound like me, Joy. She's supposed to be dragging me kicking
into the twentieth century.

Joy I've been force-feeding Jack T. S. Eliot, but even Eliot can be lazy.
"When the evening is spread out against the sky, Like a patient etherized
upon a table." What kind of image is that? He could just as easily have
written, "Like a cocktail sausage upon a tray."

Riley is beginning to feel excluded

Riley Congratulations, Jack. You seem to have found a soul-mate.

Lewis I thought you believed we didn't have souls, Christopher.

Riley Well now, you see, I regard the soul as an essentially feminine
accessory. "Anima". Quite different from "animus", the male variant.
This is how I explain the otherwise puzzling difference between the sexes.
Where men have intellect, women have soul.

Joy Professor Riley, as you know, I'm an American, and different cultures
have different modes of discourse. I need a little guidance here. Are you
being offensive, or merely stupid?

Lewis, Harrington, Oakley, and Warnie laugh

Riley pulls a face at Lewis, rather put out, but trying to laugh it off

Lewis Serves you right, Christopher. Don't be such a bully.

Riley I feel like calling for police protection. Where on earth did you find
her?

Harrington Tell me, Mrs Gresham, how do you find England?

Joy Cold. Dull.

Riley How very perceptive. How original.

Joy And I don't much care for the weather, either. Will you excuse me, Jack?
Reverend Harrington, Dr Oakley, Professor Riley, it's been my pleasure.

*Joy leaves them, but does not exit. She goes into the outer set, which we
understand is another room, and there re-reads an air-mail letter that arrived
earlier in the day. Her brisk departure has the effect of breaking up the little
party*

Harrington Thanks for the drinks, Jack.

Riley takes Lewis aside

Riley Jack, she's simply ghastly. You must get rid of her.

Lewis Oh, come on, Christopher. Just because she bit you back.

Riley Good Lord, I don't mind that. But she's got her hooks into you. You
must see that.

Lewis Christopher, she's a married woman, and she's a committed Christian. That may not warm the cockles of your heathen heart, but it does mean she's unlikely to have adulterous designs on me.

Riley Never send to know for whom the wedding bell tolls, Jack.

Lewis Look at you. All worked up over nothing. Fear not, she's harmless. And after Christmas, she sails back to New York.

Riley Beware Christmas, Jack. Look what happened to Scrooge.

Lewis Happy Christmas, Christopher.

Riley Easy to say, Jack. Easy to say.

Lewis Happy Christmas, Harry.

Oakley Happy Christmas, Jack.

Lewis Good-night, Maurice.

Riley, Oakley and Harrington exit. Warnie sees them out, taking the tray of tea items and glasses and does not return

Lewis crosses the stage to join Joy, as she stands reading her letter

Lewis Sorry about Christopher. It's nothing personal. Just how he is.

Joy It's not important.

Lewis realizes that something in her letter is absorbing her attention

Lewis Letter from home?

Joy Yes.

Lewis Bad news?

Joy In a way.

Lewis Anything I can do?

Joy I'm not sure. (*She falls silent*)

Lewis What is it?

Joy If I was back home and this was happening, I'd write to you to tell me what to do. I could say it in a letter.

Lewis That's easy. (*He takes a chair and turns it so that its back is to Joy. Then he sits, where she can't see him*) Tell me like a letter. Off you go. "Dear Mr Lewis . . .'

Joy falls in with his suggestion, at first tentatively, then with increasing feeling and fluency

Joy Dear Mr Lewis. My husband has just written to me to tell me that he's fallen in love with another woman. Her name is Renee. He wants me to give him a divorce, so that he can marry her. (*She takes up the letter and reads from it*) "Renee and I are in love, and have been since about the middle of August. If it had not been for our love I could not have come through this summer with as little anguish as I have, for things have been rough financially." Perhaps you wonder if I knew about Renee. The answer is no. But Renee is not the first.

Lewis Do you love your husband?

Joy I don't know how to answer that one. Bill's very talented, he wants to do right by everyone, he's a good man at heart, and I guess I love him. Bill's an alcoholic, he's compulsively unfaithful, he's sometimes violent, and I guess

I haven't loved him for years. Once he broke a bottle over Douglas's head. Two days later he said, "When have you ever known me do an unkind thing?" (*She begins to weep*) He's worn me out. That's the truth of it. The only thing that's new is he wants a divorce.

Lewis I had no idea.

Joy How could you? People never know about other people's lives. You have to live it to know it. Sorry. You don't agree with that.

Lewis Contrary to popular opinion, I don't know everything.

Joy recovers herself slowly

Joy A lot of good things have come out of my life with Bill. We were happy at the beginning. And there's Douglas. And there's something else, too. Something that happened to me, that was very important, that in a strange way I owe to Bill. Something I don't talk about. But I'd like to tell you. If you don't mind.

Lewis Tell me.

Joy Maybe you'll say I made it up. I don't think so. It only lasted thirty seconds, maybe less, but it changed everything for me. I've been turning into a different person ever since.

Lewis What happened?

Joy We were living in Westchester County. Bill was working in the city—in New York. One day, he phoned from his office, said he was losing control of his mind, he wasn't ever coming home. Bang, he put down the phone. That was it. I had a small baby. I was all alone. I had no idea what to do. I put the baby to bed, and I waited. He didn't come. Round about midnight, I broke down. I never felt so helpless in my life. I was downstairs, the baby was upstairs, asleep. I was crying. Then there was someone else in the room. Just for a few seconds, maybe half a minute. I knew it was a real person. More real than real. So real that everything else became like shadows. I said something. I've no idea what. I guess I was just saying, OK then. OK.

She looks up at Lewis and sees that he understands

Bill came home three days later.

Lewis Did you tell him?

Joy Yes, I told him. He believed me. He said, "I wish God would come to me." I'll say this for Bill, he has an open mind. He just can't keep any one thing in it for long.

Lewis Are you going to go back?

Joy Where else can I go?

Lewis What about the divorce?

Joy Marriage isn't just a legal contract.

Lewis No.

Joy We'd still be married, in the eyes of God.

Lewis Yes.

Joy And I wouldn't be free to marry anyone else.

Lewis No.

Joy No, I know. I've read your writings on the subject. Many times.

Lewis says nothing. He can't tell her what she wants to hear

It seems I don't need any advice after all, since I don't have a wide range of choices.

Lewis Is this woman living with him in your house?

Joy I guess so.

Lewis And that's where you're going back to?

Joy Where else can I go?

Lewis And later?

Joy I don't know. I'm sorry to burden you with all this. It's not your problem. Don't worry. I'll be all right. I always have been.

Lewis I wish there was some way I could help.

Joy There is.

He looks up, almost frightened to hear what she has to say

Lewis Yes?

Joy Be my friend.

Lewis I'm that already.

Joy I know. Thank you. I'm just going to go upstairs now . . .

On the point of further tears, Joy hurries out

Lewis looks after her, for a moment or two. Then he too rises and exits, in a different direction

The Lights change. It is morning

Warnie enters, carrying the breakfast tray as he did earlier, and his newspaper. He pours out two cups of coffee

Lewis enters, carrying the morning mail

Warnie Morning, Jack.

Lewis Morning. Two for you.

Lewis sits at his desk. The bachelor routine has returned. After a while, and without taking their eyes off their reading, they have one of their non-committal conversations

Warnie You miss her, don't you?

Lewis Things are quieter now.

Warnie I'm afraid I'm not much of a talker.

Lewis One of your many virtues.

Warnie Is she coming back?

Lewis No, no. Why should she come back?

An interval of silence

I haven't really thanked you, Warnie.

Warnie What for?

Lewis You've been very tolerant. Very considerate.

Warnie Any friend of yours, Jack.

Lewis I know.

The doorbell rings. Lewis calls out, without rising, or even turning his attention from what he is writing

That'll be Christopher. Door's open, Christopher.

*Warnie looks at his watch, a little surprised at this early visit, and then goes
back to reading the paper*

> *Riley enters, carrying a typescript. He looks round with mock trepidation*

What's the matter with you, Christopher?

Riley Is it safe to come in? *La belle* dame *sans merci*? (*He pronounces "dame"
in the American manner*)

Lewis You know perfectly well she's gone back to New York.

Riley puts the typescript on Lewis's desk before him

Riley Tom's latest, as promised. The only copy.

Lewis Any good?

Riley Not bad. If he wasn't a friend, I'd say pretty good. (*He goes to Warnie*)
Morning, Warnie.

Warnie Morning, Christopher.

Riley (*turning to Lewis*) Just as well, perhaps, Jack.

Lewis What's just as well?

Riley The return of the native.

Lewis What are you trying to say?

Riley You know how people talk.

Lewis To be honest, Christopher, I don't know and I don't care. A like-
minded man and woman are entitled to be friends, it seems to me. I don't
see why I should disqualify half the human race just because they're also
available for other purposes.

Riley I won't quarrel with that. Friendship for ever.

Lewis It's all love or sex these days. Friendship is almost as quaint and out-
dated a notion as chastity. Soon friends will be like the elves and the pixies;
fabulous mythical creatures from a distant past.

Riley Too optimistic, Jack. Friendship will be made illegal, clearly. "The
accused has been found guilty of gross public friendship. I hereby pass
sentence of five years marriage, with no remission."

They chuckle. Warnie puts down his paper, and rises from his chair

Warnie No news, of course. Never is.

Riley Shall we see you in hall, Warnie? Like old times?

Warnie Like old times, Christopher. Why not?

> *Warnie exits*

*Riley sits down in his chair, and picks up the newspaper. Lewis becomes
reflective*

Lewis Tell me something, Christopher. How can I put this? Would you say
that you were . . . content?

Riley I am as I am. The world is as it is. My contentment or otherwise has
very little to do with it.

Lewis You don't ever feel a sense of waste?

Riley Of course. All life is waste. Remember, I don't have your faith in divine re-cycling.

Lewis I've always found this a trying time of the year. The leaves not yet out. Mud everywhere you go. The frosty mornings gone, and the sunny mornings not yet come. The air dank and unhealthy. Give me blizzards and frozen pipes, but not this nothing time. Not this waiting-room of a world.

Riley May will come, Jack. And June. And July.

Lewis And I have two books to finish, and six talks to write, and letters, letters, letters. (*He turns to his work, waiting on his desk*)

Riley rises from his chair, and watches him with some sympathy, understanding him better than his friend realizes. Then he exits

Lewis finds it difficult to concentrate, but after a few moments, he gets into the way of it

As he works, Joy enters

He does not see her. She stands still, watching Lewis work, but does not speak. Lewis becomes aware that he is not alone. He raises his head, listening without turning round

Joy Remember me?

Lewis Joy! (*He turns round and sees her*) What are you doing here?

Joy The door was open.

Lewis But . . . ?

Joy We live here now. Douglas and I.

Lewis Here? In Oxford?

Joy Yes, but don't worry. We have our own house this time. We'll be no trouble at all.

Lewis stares at her, still too stunned to be polite

Would you like a cup of tea?

Lewis Yes.

Joy Then you're going to have to make it. This is your house.

Lewis Of course. Yes. I'm sorry, Joy, I'm a little confused. Why didn't you write?

Joy What for? To ask permission?

Lewis No, no. But . . . when did you decide this? How did you find a house? How was it all arranged?

Joy And what have I done with Bill? We're divorced. No more Bill. No more America.

Lewis I see.

Joy Do you mind?

Lewis Why should I mind?

Joy I don't know. You might.

Lewis No. I don't mind.

Joy That's all right, then.

They walk forward, out of the study. The screen falls

So tell me the news.

Lewis What news?

Joy Don't tell me that time has stood still since I've been away.

Lewis Gone by at a slow amble, perhaps. I may be offered a chair at Cambridge, if you call that news. Professor of Medieval and Renaissance Literature.

Joy Will you take it?

Lewis Probably.

Joy You'd leave Oxford?

Lewis Only to teach. I'd go on living here. Cambridge is a chilly sort of town.

Joy So you won't be moving out just as I move in? (*She makes a joke of this, but she is secretly relieved that he is not leaving Oxford*)

He looks at her with affection

Lewis I really am very—very surprised to see you, you know.

Joy I think you're overdoing the surprise a bit, Jack. I wasn't dead. I was only in America.

Lewis Yes, of course. But you see, I've been thinking about— (*he hesitates to say it; then decides he will*) I've been thinking about you.

Joy I am honoured.

Lewis Yes. I was thinking about you. And, there you were.

Joy Here I am. Present tense. Present, and tense.

Lewis I really am very glad to see you again.

Joy Thank you. So this is it.

He has gone a little further than he intended, and changes the subject to the safer, more neutral matter now facing them. During the following speech, the screen rises, to reveal Joy's house. It is empty but for the packing cases

Lewis Moving house is a sort of revolution, I always think. The old order is overthrown, a new order waits to be born. One wakes up facing a strange way, one's books are all in strange places, and there's nowhere to hang one's dressing-gown.

Joy When did you last move house?

Lewis Twenty-five years ago. Thank God that's over.

Joy laughs. She goes to work on the packing cases. Lewis looks about the room

Joy I don't know why I brought all this stuff.

Lewis What is it?

Joy My uncollected works. How can I have written all this stuff?

Lewis I'm sure it's nothing to be ashamed of.

Joy You haven't read it. Nor will you.

Lewis What can I do to help?

Joy Books into shelves.

Lewis takes the books and starts reading one of them. Joy watches him

Are you sure you want to do this?

Lewis I said I'd help. Any particular order?

Joy Put them anywhere they'll fit. I'll sort them out later.

They work on in silence for a few moments

Lewis How does Bill feel about you coming to live in England?

Joy I don't think he likes it. On the other hand, he can only afford to give me sixty dollars a month, and England's cheaper.

Lewis How much is that? It doesn't sound enough.

Joy We'll manage.

Lewis If you find things are getting tight, you will let me know, won't you?

Joy I don't want to take your money, Jack.

Lewis Don't be silly. That's what friends are for.

Joy We are friends, aren't we?

Lewis We most certainly are.

Joy's attention is caught by a newspaper in which her possessions have been packed. The headline announces Princess Margaret's dramatic "duty before love" decision not to marry Group-Captain Peter Townsend

Joy "Should Princess Margaret have followed the dictates of her heart?" "Group-Captain Peter Townsend's lips are sealed, but his hands are shaking." "She chose duty before love." So what do you think about the heartbreak princess?

Lewis The dictates of her heart! It almost sounds like a higher authority, doesn't it? All it means is, doing what she feels like doing.

Joy I knew you'd be on the side of duty.

Lewis I don't pretend it's an easy decision.

Joy Easy it's not. (*She returns to the business of unpacking*)

Lewis It's a big change for you, this.

Joy England?

Lewis Yes.

Joy If it turns out to be a mistake, I'll have lost very little. But I do hope it works out for Douglas.

Lewis What made you decide?

Joy I had to go somewhere. And I like England.

Lewis And it's cheaper.

Joy I like Oxford.

Lewis All those warm-hearted dons, with their love of female company.

Joy I can handle that.

Lewis The balmy English weather.

Joy I like the way Oxford's been here a long time. Not everything is the impulse of the moment. I like being among educated people. And I like living in the same town as you. Do you mind?

Lewis My dear Joy, I don't own Oxford.

Joy Do you mind?

Lewis Of course I don't mind. Why should I?

Joy You know what I mean, Jack.

Lewis I'm delighted to have you as a neighbour.

She looks at him

Why are you looking at me like that?

Joy Like what?

Lewis As if I'm lying to you. Why should I lie to you? I mean what I say.
Joy I know that. But you don't say it all, do you?
Lewis One can't say it all. It would take too long.
Joy All right, Jack. But I trust you to tell me anything I need to know.

Again, she returns to the unpacking. Lewis puzzles over what she has just said

Lewis What sort of thing do you need to know?
Joy I want to stay friends with you, Jack. I need to know anything that would make that hard for you.
Lewis I see.
Joy We might as well know where we are.
Lewis Best to have things out in the open, you think?
Joy That's how I like it.
Lewis You never can really tell what's going on between people, can you? People jump to conclusions. Sometimes it makes me quite angry the way people aren't allowed to be . . . well, just friends.
Joy Like us, you mean.
Lewis Like us. I don't mean to say that friendship is a small thing. As a matter of fact, I rate it as one of this life's most precious gifts.
Joy But——
Lewis But it shouldn't be turned into a watered-down version of something it is not.
Joy Such as . . .
Lewis Such as, well, to give you one example, romantic love. Which nowadays is just about the only emotion men and women are permitted to feel for each other. Though that's not to say that friendship isn't, in its way——
Joy A kind of love.
Lewis A kind of love. I knew you'd understand.
Joy I understand better than that, Jack. You are a bachelor and I am a divorced woman. Some people might suppose you to have some idea of marrying me. You have no such idea. I am to have no false expectations. You want to have this "out in the open" because you care about me and don't want me to be hurt. Have I understood you correctly?
Lewis You are extraordinary.
Joy Uh-huh.
Lewis I don't know what to say.
Joy It's OK. I just said it. Wasn't so hard, was it?
Lewis I'm not used to this . . . Whatever it is.
Joy Naming names. That's all it is.
Lewis Yes.
Joy So now you don't need to be afraid of me, do you?
Lewis Good Lord, I was never afraid of you, Joy.

She looks at him. He shrugs and smiles

Joy I really do appreciate your help, Jack.
Lewis The least I can do. Is there anything else I can do to help?
Joy I don't want to exhaust your good will.

Lewis No fear of that. I think it grows by being drawn on.

Joy If I asked for something, and you couldn't give it, you would say no, wouldn't you? I mean, just, no. No guilt, no evasion, no running away.

Lewis I hope so. I don't think you'd ask for anything beyond my power to give.

Joy No. Not beyond your power.

Lewis There's something in particular, is there?

Joy Yes, there is. There is something you could do that would help me a great deal.

Lewis I think I know what it is. You want me to put the kettle on.

Lewis exits. A couple of beats. Joy follows him

The screen falls

Warnie enters, with a deckchair, and settles down to read, downstage to one side

Lewis enters with a deckchair of his own, and does likewise

Warnie (*after a few moments*) So she's settled over here for good, has she?

Lewis Who knows? For the foreseeable future.

Warnie Why Oxford?

Lewis Why not Oxford? Dreaming spires, and so forth.

Warnie You know how it looks, don't you, Jack?

Lewis I know.

Neither of them have taken their noses out of their books. There follows a short silence

She's a good friend to me. That's all.

Warnie nods

Warnie Is that how she sees it?

Lewis I wouldn't presume to raise the matter.

Warnie No. Of course not.

Another short silence

Lewis Oh, Warnie. There is something you should know.

Warnie What's that, Jack?

Lewis I've agreed to marry her.

Warnie You have?

Lewis Yes. Seemed like the right thing to do.

Warnie You astound me. No, I mean . . .

Lewis It's all right. Nothing's going to change. I'm not really going to marry Joy.

Warnie You're not?

Lewis What I have agreed to do is extend my British citizenship to her, so that she can go on living in England.

Warnie By marrying her.

Lewis Only technically.

Warnie You're marrying Joy technically?

During the following, Lewis rises and takes up his chair

Lewis A true marriage is a declaration before God, not before some government official. Joy will keep her own name. She will go on living in her own house. We will all go on living here exactly as before. No-one will even know the marriage has taken place, apart from you, Somerset House, and the Department of Immigration. It's nothing more than a bureaucratic formality. See you at tea.

Lewis exits, taking his deckchair with him. Thunder is heard

Warnie Oh blast.

The screen rises to reveal a Register Office, where Joy waits, before a Registrar, Clerk and witness

Warnie joins them

Lewis enters, hurriedly and late, carrying a pile of books

Lewis I'm so sorry.

Registrar Mr Lewis. Please be seated. (*He opens a book*) We'll proceed at once. (*Reading from the book*) "Before you are joined in matrimony, I have to remind you of the solemn and binding character of the vows you are about to make. Marriage according to the law of this country is the union of one man with one woman, voluntarily entered into for life, to the exclusion of all others." Now we proceed to the declarations. If you'd both stand. Mr Lewis, if you'll repeat after me, "I call upon these persons here present."

Lewis speaks in an unduly clear voice

Lewis I call upon these persons here present.
Registrar To witness that I, Clive Staples Lewis.
Lewis To witness that I, Clive Staples Lewis.
Registrar Do take thee, Helen Joy Davidman.
Lewis Do take thee, Helen Joy Davidman.
Registrar To be my lawful wedded wife.
Lewis To be my lawful wedded wife.
Registrar Miss Davidman, if you'll repeat after me. "I call upon these persons here present."

Joy's responses are more muted

Joy I call upon these persons here present.
Registrar To witness that I, Helen Joy Davidman.
Joy To witness that I, Helen Joy Davidman.
Registrar Do take thee, Clive Staples Lewis.
Joy Do take thee, Clive Staples Lewis.
Registrar To be my lawful wedded husband.
Joy To be my lawful wedded husband.
Registrar Do we have a ring?

Lewis ⎱ (*together*) No. Sorry.
Joy ⎰

The whole affair is very awkward and embarrassing

Registrar No ring. Very well. If you'll please both sign the register. Before you sign, be careful to check that all the details are exactly correct.

Joy signs the register quickly. Lewis studies it almost too carefully before signing. Warnie, a witness, the Registrar and Clerk all sign the register. The Clerk puts the certificate in an envelope

Clerk Mrs Lewis. Mrs Lewis.

Joy comes and takes the envelope

Registrar May I be the first to congratulate you, and wish you every happiness in your life together.
Lewis Well, do you know, that's most kind of you.

The Registrar exits with the Clerk and witness

Lewis, Joy and Warnie walk downstage, and the screen falls behind them. They have come out into rain

Joy What a terrible day.
Lewis That's that, then.
Joy Can I invite you both back for a drink?
Lewis I simply can't, Joy. Please forgive me, but I must get back to work. I really shouldn't be here at all.
Joy Of course, Jack. Off you go.

Lewis exits

Warnie I would be most grateful for a drink, Joy.
Joy That's kind of you, Warnie. I must admit, I found that an unusual experience.
Warnie Yes. You must forgive Jack.
Joy Oh, I'm getting to know him a little now. I think I understand him. I'm very grateful to him.
Warnie Nobody is to know, he tells me.
Joy That's right. Best that way.
Warnie What he actually said was, it will be as if it never happened.
Joy Yes.
Warnie Odd business.
Joy It is that.
Warnie Jack plays safe, you see. Always has.
Joy I do rather need that drink.

Warnie and Joy exit

The screen rises to reveal Joy's house

Lewis is there with Douglas, who is in his pyjamas

Lewis So how do you like it here?
Douglas Not much. Mom says we don't have to stay if we don't like it.
Lewis So you're seeing if you like it.
Douglas Except I don't.
Lewis What about your mother?
Douglas I guess she likes it.
Lewis And you want to stay with her?
Douglas Yes. Have you met my dad?
Lewis No.
Douglas He's OK, my dad. But I love Mom the best.

Joy enters

Joy Douglas. Bed.

Douglas turns to go

Douglas Night, Mr Lewis.
Lewis Good-night, Douglas.
Joy One chapter.

Douglas exits

Lewis He's so obedient. I like him.
Joy He likes you.
Lewis He doesn't seem very impressed by England.
Joy He'll get used to it.
Lewis So this is it, is it? Land of Hope and Glory?
Joy I think so. I'm happier here than I've been in a long time.
Lewis That's good.
Joy Mostly because of you, Jack. One good friend can make all the difference.
Lewis You're not getting sick of the sight of me, then?
Joy Not yet. Though heaven knows what the neighbours think.
Lewis The worst, I've no doubt.
Joy Don't you sometimes burst to share the joke?
Lewis What joke?
Joy Well. Here's the neighbours thinking we're unmarried and up to all sorts of wickedness, while all along we're married and up to nothing at all.

She sees that her joke makes him uneasy

Only technically married, of course.
Lewis Do you think I come round too often?
Joy Too often for what? We're friends. That's what we agreed. Good friends.

Lewis prepares to leave. She gets his coat, and helps him on with it. Her hands rest on his shoulders. He moves away

I'm not going to talk about it any more. You get that twitchy look in your eyes, and you start feeling in your coat pockets, as if there's something there you have to find.

Lewis is doing just as she describes. He stops, and removes his hands from his pockets

Lewis You know me too well.
Joy Don't say that. Just say, I know you.
Lewis You know me.
Douglas (*off*) Mom! I'm ready!
Joy I'll be right there.
Lewis I'll say goodnight, then.

As Lewis is about to leave, a sudden pain strikes her

Joy Ah!
Lewis What is it?
Joy I don't know. It's all right. It's gone again.
Lewis Well, good-night, then.
Joy Good-night, Jack.

He pats her on one arm and they exchange a peck on the cheek

   Lewis exits

Joy stands looking after him. Then she turns to go to Douglas. Her body twists, and her mouth opens in a silent scream. Suddenly, she crumples to the floor

CURTAIN

ACT II

The screen is down

Lewis enters, and speaks to the audience, as he did at the beginning of the play. As the talk proceeds, there are signs that he is using it to persuade himself of a belief that is beginning to slide. However, at this stage, he hardly realizes this process himself

Lewis Recently a friend of mine, a brave and Christian woman, collapsed in terrible pain. One minute she seemed fit and well. The next minute she was in agony. She is now in hospital, suffering from advanced bone cancer, and almost certainly dying. Why?

I find it hard to believe that God loves her. If you love someone, you don't want them to suffer. You can't bear it. You want to take their suffering on to yourself. If even I feel like that, why doesn't God? Not just once in history, on the cross, but again and again? Today. Now.

It's at times like this that we have to remind ourselves of the very core of the Christian faith. There are other worlds than this. This world, that seems so real, is no more than the shadow of the life to come. If we believe that all is well in this present life, if we can imagine nothing more satisfactory than this present life, then we are under a dangerous illusion. All is not well. Believe me, all is not well.

His present experience, Joy's suffering, breaks through the familiar pattern of his lecture

Suffering . . . By suffering . . . Through suffering, we release our hold on the toys of this world, and know that our true good lies in another world.

But after we have suffered so much, must we still suffer more? And more?

He has no answer to this question, which torments him. All he can do is repeat his familiar lines, wanting to believe them

We are like blocks of stone, out of which the sculptor carves the forms of men. The blows of his chisel, which hurt us so much, are what make us perfect.

He turns aside, to hide his feeling

Warnie enters, with Douglas. He sits Douglas down on a chair, and comes to Lewis

Douglas reads the book he is carrying

Warnie How is she?

Lewis Not good. Not good.

Warnie I'm sorry, Jack.

Lewis I want her to get well again, you see.

Warnie Of course you do. We all do.

Lewis What a dangerous world we live in, Warnie. How full of cutting edges. They give her morphine, you know. No morphine for me.

Warnie You've been up all night, Jack. You must get some sleep.

Lewis I can't sleep. I've never felt more awake in my life. (*He moves restlessly about*) This isn't the right time, you see, Warnie. It's too soon.

Warnie Too soon for what, Jack?

Lewis I haven't had time, you see.

Warnie Time for what, Jack?

Lewis Time to talk. Time to get to know her. Time to . . . say things.

Now Warnie understands

Warnie It doesn't take long.

Lewis No. I suppose not.

Warnie Whatever it is, I should just say it.

Lewis Would you, Warnie? You're quite right, of course. But it's difficult, you see.

Warnie Yes. I do see that.

Lewis I just want her to be well again. That's all.

The screen rises, revealing a Hospital Room

 Joy lies in a bed. A Nurse comes forward to collect Douglas

Lewis goes to Douglas to prepare him

 You know she's not strong, don't you? She's in very good hands. Very good hands. She sleeps a lot. You mustn't mind. Sleep's good for her. Sleep, the great healer.

Warnie Are you a bun-man, Douglas? Like buns, do you?

Douglas Yes.

Warnie We'll have a bun-tea later. I shall like that.

Nurse Douglas, you can see your mother now.

The Nurse takes Douglas to Joy's bedside

Lewis That's *The Magician's Nephew* he's carrying around with him.

Warnie Yes. I noticed.

Lewis The boy travels to Narnia, and picks a magic apple, and brings it back to his dying mother, and makes her well again.

Warnie Poor kid.

Lewis I'm a fraud, Warnie.

 A Doctor enters, and comes to Lewis

Doctor Mr Lewis.

Lewis Ah, Doctor. Any change?

Doctor She's been sleeping. Otherwise, nothing to report, really.

Lewis How much has she been told?

Doctor She's been told that the cancer has eaten through her left femur. That she has a malignant tumour in one breast. She knows it's serious. How can she not know? Her hip bone snapped like a frozen twig.

Lewis So suddenly. I don't understand. How can this have happened with no warning?

Doctor I'm told there had been occasional pain before.

Lewis Everyone has occasional pain.

Doctor That's often how it goes, I'm afraid.

Lewis I don't understand it.

Doctor To tell you the truth, Mr Lewis, nor do we.

Warnie How bad is it?

Lewis She's likely to die.

Doctor That's putting it more starkly than I would choose. I don't pretend to be able to prophesy the future.

Lewis No. But it's true, isn't it?

Doctor The cancer is very advanced.

Inside the Hospital Room, Douglas kisses his mother and leaves her. He comes out into the corridor

Lewis Right. Thank you, Doctor.

The Doctor and Nurse exit

Warnie (*taking charge of Douglas*) Buns, buns. That's what's needed. There must be some buns somewhere.

Warnie and Douglas exit

Lewis walks on alone into the hospital room, where Joy lies in bed, weakened by pain and by pain-killers

Lewis Hallo, Joy.

Joy Hallo, Jack.

Lewis How's the pain?

Joy Kind of pushy.

Lewis Don't talk if it hurts.

Joy Did you visit before?

Lewis Yes. A couple of times.

Joy I thought so.

Lewis They're going to operate on the broken hip tomorrow.

Joy I'm sorry, Jack. I didn't mean you to have all this bother.

Lewis Tush, woman. You're the one who's having the bother.

Joy What I mean is, I don't expect you to worry about me.

Lewis Oh? And who do you expect to worry about you?

Joy You know what I'm trying to say.

Lewis Who else should be worrying about you but me? You are my wife.

Joy Technically.

Lewis Then I shall worry about you technically.

Joy Just how much is there to worry about, Jack? They won't tell me.

Lewis That's because they're not sure themselves.

Joy Tell me, Jack.

Lewis I don't know any more than they do, Joy.

Joy Please.

Lewis (*after a pause*) They expect you to die.

Joy Thank you. (*Having got what she wanted, she pauses to regain strength*) What do you say, Jack? I'm a Jew. Divorced. Broke. And I'm dying of cancer. Do I get a discount?

Lewis Oh, Joy.

Joy You know something? You seem different. You look at me properly now.

Lewis Didn't I before?

Joy Not properly.

Lewis I don't want to lose you.

Joy I don't want to be lost.

Lewis Please.

He holds out his hand. She gives him her hand. He holds it, and strokes it

Joy Can I say whatever I want, Jack?

Lewis Yes.

Joy Anything?

Lewis Yes.

Joy You know anyway.

Lewis Yes.

Joy I'm still going to say it.

Lewis You say it.

Joy I love you, Jack.

He seems about to respond with a declaration of his own. But it does not quite come out

Lewis Better now?

Joy Better. Do you mind?

Lewis No.

A spasm of pain passes through her

He watches Joy in pain. He can't bear it. He goes looking for a Nurse

Nurse! Nurse!

A Nurse enters

The Nurse examines Joy

Nurse I'll fetch the doctor.

The Nurse leaves

Lewis holds Joy's hand as she suffers

The Doctor enters at last, and comes to Joy's side. The screen falls. When the screen is in place Lewis and the Doctor exit

Harrington and Riley enter. They stroll across the stage together, gravely discussing their friend's situation

Harrington Poor Jack. It's knocked him completely off-balance.
Riley Looks bad, does it?
Harrington Oh yes. They don't expect her to live.
Riley Sad business.
Harrington Has he said anything to you?
Riley About her?
Harrington Yes.
Riley No. Nothing.

Oakley crosses the stage

Oakley Morning, Harry.
Harrington Morning, Maurice.
Oakley Christopher.
Riley Maurice.

Oakley exits

Harrington I don't suppose you were listening in to the wireless last night?
Riley Jack wasn't on, was he?
Harrington No, no. It was *Twenty Questions*. You're not a Gilbert Harding appreciator, then?
Riley His fascination has eluded me so far.

Harrington chuckles at the memory

Harrington Oh, he's something quite tremendous. The other day he said, "When I hear the words 'ethical' and 'artistic', I say fiddle-de-dee and tiddley-push."
Riley Ye-es. That is rather good.

Lewis enters, in a distracted state

Harrington Do you listen to *Twenty Questions*, Jack?
Lewis *Twenty Questions*? No. I can't say I do, Harry.
Riley Other things to think about, eh, Jack.
Lewis Other things. Yes.

There is a short awkward pause. Neither Riley nor Harrington feels quite able to bring up the subject of Joy. Lewis resolves the awkwardness by starting to speak of her, without introduction, as if she is as much in their minds as she is in his

She's in very good hands. She sleeps a good deal. Sleep is good, don't you think? Sleep, the great healer.
Harrington Great healer.
Riley I'm so sorry about all this, Jack.
Lewis Yes. It's all come too soon, you see. Her affairs aren't in order. What's to happen to Douglas, for example?
Harrington I suppose his father——
Lewis She doesn't want that. He drinks, you see.

Harrington I don't really see what you can do about that.

Lewis Do you think I should take the boy in?

Harrington There must be relatives, Jack. I mean, it's not as if . . .

Lewis Not as if what?

Harrington Well, she's your friend, of course, but she's not . . . well, family.

Lewis Not my wife?

Harrington gives a nervous laugh at such a prospect

Harrington No. Of course not.

Lewis Of course not. Impossible. Unthinkable.

Harrington I only meant——

Lewis How could Joy be my wife? I'd have to love her, wouldn't I? I'd have to care more for her than for anyone else in this world. I'd have to be suffering the torments of the damned at the prospect of losing her.

Harrington is awed by Lewis's passionate outburst

Harrington I'm sorry, Jack. I didn't know.

Lewis Nor did I, Harry. (*Suddenly, his manner changes. He becomes calm, almost businesslike*) I'm going to marry Joy. I've made up my mind. I want you to marry us properly, before God.

Harrington is now embarrassed professionally as well as personally

Harrington I think it would be best if we talked about this later, Jack.

Lewis We don't have a later.

Harrington Still. It's not entirely plain sailing, is it? (*He looks to Riley for support*)

Riley I think Harry's trying to say it's against the rules.

Harrington She's a divorced woman, Jack. The bishop would never let me.

Lewis stares at him as if he understands, but when he speaks it is clear that nothing Harrington has said has gone in

Lewis I'm going to marry her. If you won't do it, I'll find someone who will.

Harrington I don't make the rules.

Riley Jack. I can't pretend to understand what's happening to you, but if this is what you want, I wish you both happy.

Harrington I'm really sorry, Jack.

Lewis That's all right, Harry. I understand. (*He goes towards the Hospital Room*)

Riley and Harrington exit as the screen rises

Lewis goes back to Joy's bedside. She is alone

It's me again.

Joy Did you go?

Lewis I went. And I came back.

Joy This dope they give me. I get confused.

Lewis Does it help the pain?

Joy Oh yes. It's the strangest sensation. Like the pain's still going on down there, but it's nothing to do with me.

Lewis Is your mind clear now?
Joy How would I know? Try me.
Lewis What's fifty-eight take away forty-one?

She wrestles with the sum

Joy Oh, Jack! Seventeen?
Lewis That's how old I was when you were born.
Joy I was a baby. You were almost a man. For a while back there, I thought I might just catch you up. But here I am, back to being a baby again. (*This long speech wears her out, and she closes her eyes*)

Lewis looks lovingly down at her

Lewis Joy?
Joy Still here.
Lewis I'm going to marry you, Joy. I'm going to marry you before God and the world.
Joy You don't have to, Jack.
Lewis I want to. It's what I want.
Joy Make an honest woman of me.
Lewis Not you, Joy. It's me who hasn't been honest. Look what it takes to make me see sense.
Joy You think I overdid it?
Lewis Don't leave me, Joy.

She smiles. The morphine makes her sleepy. For a moment, she closes her eyes

Joy Jack. About this marrying.
Lewis I'll find a way. I promise.
Joy Back home, we have a quaint old custom. When the guy has made up his mind he wants to marry the girl, he asks her. It's called proposing.
Lewis It's the same here.
Joy Did I miss it?

He takes her hand and kisses it

Lewis Will you marry this foolish, frightened, old man, who needs you more than he can bear to say, and loves you even though he hardly knows how?
Joy OK. Just this once.

> *Douglas enters. He stands in silence, watching*
>
> *Warnie enters, accompanied by a young Priest, who carries a service book. The Priest goes to the bedside, and opens his book*

Lewis holds Joy's hand. Joy is fully awake now, and though weak, radiantly happy. She speaks the marriage vow clearly and steadily

I, Joy, take thee, Jack.
Priest To have and to hold, from this day forward.

Behind them, the Lights come up in the Other World space, and the wardrobe doors swing open of their own accord. Only Douglas sees this. He turns and stares

Joy To have and to hold, from this day forward.
Priest For better, for worse.
Joy For better, for worse.

Douglas moves softly away from the group towards the Other World space, as the familiar ritual continues

Priest For richer, for poorer.
Joy For richer, for poorer.
Priest In sickness and in health.
Joy In sickness and in health.
Priest To love, cherish, and obey.
Joy To love, cherish, and obey.
Priest Till death us do part.
Joy Till death us do part.

Douglas has now entered the Other World space, and holds up his hand to a tree that grows there, and picks from it a glowing magic apple

Warnie steps forward and gives Lewis a ring. Lewis puts the ring on Joy's finger

Priest With this ring I thee wed.
Lewis With this ring I thee wed.
Priest With my body I thee worship.
Lewis With my body I thee worship.
Priest With all my worldly goods I thee endow.
Lewis With all my worldly goods I thee endow.

Douglas carries the magic apple back into the Hospital Room and kneels at the foot of her bed

Priest In the name of the Father.
Lewis In the name of the Father.
Priest And of the son.
Lewis And of the son.
Priest And of the Holy Ghost.
Lewis And of the Holy Ghost.
Priest Amen.
Lewis Amen.

Lewis takes Joy's hands in his and bows his head over them

Priest Those whom God hath joined together, let no man put asunder. For as much as Jack and Joy have consented to enter into Holy Wedlock and have made witness of the same before God and this company, I pronounce them Man and Wife together. In the name of the Father and of the Son and of the Holy Ghost. Amen.

Joy is now asleep again

Warnie and the Priest exit

Lewis kisses Joy's forehead and moves downstage. Douglas places the magic apple in his mother's hands. Then he bends over her, and kisses her. The Lights fade on the Other World and the screen falls

Douglas exits

The Doctor enters and goes to Lewis

Time has passed

Doctor Well, Mr Lewis, I think I'm in no danger of overstating the case if I say, no news is good news. Given the seriousness of her condition, we have reason to be cautiously optimistic.

Lewis I'm sorry, Doctor, but I don't understand a word you're saying. It would help me, if you would use words I'm familiar with, like "getting better", "getting worse". "Dying."

Doctor I'm afraid none of those words meet the case. What seems to be happening is that the rate of spread of the disease is slowing down.

Lewis Is she better than she was?

Doctor She's not worse.

Lewis Is not-being-worse better than not-being-better.

Doctor Put like that, yes.

Lewis Thank you. Then she's better than she was.

Doctor Mr Lewis. You're looking at a train, standing in a station. It may not be moving right now, but trains move. That's how trains are.

Lewis What would be a good sign? People do recover from cancer. It has been known.

Doctor Any sign of returning strength. Any sign that the body is rebuilding the diseased bone.

Lewis Did you expect her to make it this far?

Doctor What can I say? Remissions do happen.

Lewis accepts this as the Doctor's attempt at encouragement

Lewis Thank you.

The Doctor exits

Lewis enters the hospital room, where Joy is now sitting up in bed. He pulls a chair to her bedside, and sits down by her. Joy is still weak, but in very good spirits

I should have brought you something, shouldn't I? Flowers. Grapes. Why grapes, I wonder?

Nurse Only five minutes, Mr Lewis.

Joy Just bring me books, Jack. I'm going crazy here. The nurse has been telling me all about her love life. She's been dating this boy for two years. Will he marry her? How far should she let him go without them being at least engaged? I'm telling you, I was almost sick with excitement. But she doesn't see him again till Saturday, so I need books.

Lewis smiles at her ready chatter. Just looking at her makes him feel happy

Lewis It strikes me you're rather better.

Joy Shh! We have to pretend we haven't noticed, or He'll take it away.

Lewis So what advice did you give the nurse?

Joy I said, give him enough to make him want the rest, then nothing till he pays up.

Lewis Poor fellow. He hasn't a chance.

Joy holds up her hand, to look at her wedding ring

Joy Jack. If I get better, do I have to give the ring back?

Lewis That's for ever, Joy. For all eternity.

Joy You don't have to feel sorry for me now.

Lewis Nor for myself. All I want is some time with you, Joy.

Joy Shh! (*She glances upwards, at God, who mustn't hear*) Speaking of Him, how did you square it?

Lewis Marrying you?

Joy Yes. You're not the sort to say, it's wrong, but I want it.

Lewis I did think about it, yes. The argument I put to myself went like this. I want to marry Joy, but if she's married to someone else, I can't. Whatever a divorce court decrees, marriage is indissoluble in the eyes of God. But you see, your husband had been married before. If marriage is indissoluble, he's still married to his first wife. If he's still married to his first wife, he can't have married you. Not in the eyes of God. He wasn't free. So you were never really married to him in the first place.

Joy laughs

Am I being too clever?

Joy You're doing fine. Just fine.

A Nurse enters, with screens to put round the bed

Nurse I said five minutes, Mr Lewis.

Lewis kisses Joy, and turns to leave

Lewis (*leaving; to the Nurse*) Good luck on Saturday.

Lewis exits, as the screen falls

Warnie and Harrington enter

Harrington Frankly, I'm worried about him. His behaviour is entirely out of character.

Warnie It's been a very great shock to him.

Harrington That's my point. I know they've become good friends——

Warnie Husband and wife.

Harrington Well, quite. I mean, what can one say? The woman is dying.

Warnie Not any more.

Harrington Not dying?

Warnie Jack says she's recovering. The cancer has stopped spreading.

Harrington is disconcerted by this information

Harrington That's very good news. Excellent news. So what will you do, Warnie?

Warnie What do you mean?

Harrington Well, if she makes a full recovery. Where will you live?
Warnie I don't know. (*This point had not occurred to him. It does now*)

Riley enters

Harrington turns to him, expecting to find an ally

Harrington Christopher. Excellent news. Mrs Gresham is not to die after all.
Riley That is good news. (*He says no more than this, but it is clear he feels deeply relieved*)
Warnie I think we must call her Mrs Lewis, you know.
Harrington If she does recover, we shall chalk it up as a victory for the power of prayer.
Riley I've never quite understood about prayer. Does God intervene in the world only when asked?
Harrington It has been known.
Riley And what are the qualifications for divine aid? Merit? Intense suffering? Persistent prayer? I mean, how does He choose?
Harrington I hardly think this is the time or the place for a theological argument.
Riley And if God knows what's best for us anyway, why do we need to ask? Doesn't He know already?

Lewis enters

Lewis Doesn't who know what?
Harrington Jack, Christopher's being Christopherish about prayer.
Lewis Prayer? I pray all the time these days. If I stopped praying, I think I'd stop living.
Harrington And God hears your prayer, doesn't He? We hear Joy's getting better.
Lewis Yes. She is.
Warnie I'm very glad, Jack.
Lewis That's not why I pray, Harry. I pray because I can't help myself. I pray because I'm helpless. I pray because the need flows out of me all the time, waking and sleeping. It doesn't change God. It changes me.
Riley Now, that I can understand. That's the first sensible thing I've heard anyone say on the subject.
Lewis She's getting better, you see. It's quite something. We mustn't expect too much, of course. Mustn't get our hopes up. Shall we go, Warnie?
Warnie Ready when you are, Jack.

Harrington and Riley exit

The screen rises to reveal the Hospital Room again. Joy's bed is behind the hospital screens. Lewis and Warnie cross to the corridor outside the Hospital Room

The Doctor enters

Lewis (*turning eagerly to the Doctor*) Well?
Doctor I think you should come and see for yourself.

Lewis See what?
Doctor She's doing rather well, all things considered.

Lewis follows the Doctor to the screened bed. Warnie stays back, not wanting to intrude. Lewis stands before the closed screens, as the Doctor draws them back. The bed is empty. Joy stands beside the bed, supported by crutches, and attended by the watchful Nurse

Lewis Rather well!
Joy Hallo, Jack.
Lewis Joy!
Joy Impressed?

He runs to her and takes her in his arms

I'm still very wonky.

He releases her and stands back to gaze in wonder at her new mobility

Lewis Show me.

She walks a few cautious steps. Warnie, the Doctor, and the Nurse clap. Lewis turns to them like a proud parent

You see that, Warnie? You see that?
Warnie Good show, Joy. Good show.
Lewis Do some more.
Doctor Slowly now.
Lewis Of course, of course. That's enough. Rest.

The Nurse helps Joy to the side of the bed. Lewis goes to the Doctor

Lewis When can I take her home?
Doctor As soon as you like. I see no reason to keep her in hospital, so long as the remission continues.
Lewis Which is how long?

The Doctor glances towards Joy

You can speak openly. She does have an interest in the matter.
Doctor It could be months. It could be weeks.
Lewis Why not years?
Doctor In such an advanced case, that would be . . . unusual. I'm sorry. You did want to know.
Lewis Right. We take what we can get. (*He goes to Joy*) How would you like to come home?
Joy Where's home, Jack?
Lewis My house. Our house. You're my wife, remember? Warnie and I are going to look after you.
Joy Have you asked Warnie?
Lewis Ah. (*He goes over to Warnie*) Warnie.
Warnie Don't worry about me, Jack. I'll sort myself out.
Lewis Sort yourself out? What do you mean?
Warnie New digs. No problem.

Lewis Do you want to?
Warnie As you wish, Jack.
Lewis I don't.
Warnie Right you are.
Lewis That's settled, then.

Warnie kisses Joy

Warnie See you at home, Joy.

Warnie exits

The Nurse steps forward and drapes a coat over Joy's shoulders. She and Lewis help Joy to rise. Lewis and Joy walk slowly DS. *He carries her suitcase*

Joy Thank you for everything, Nurse.
Lewis Yes, thank you for everything.

The screen falls behind them and the Nurse exits with the doctor

Joy Not bad?
Lewis Not bad. Now I don't want to hear any talk of miracles.
Joy Why not? It's a miracle to me.
Lewis Miracles frighten me.
Joy Take it when it's offered, I say.
Lewis I'm frightened of loving God too much for giving you back to me.
   That way, I could just as easily hate God, later.
Joy Don't be so hard on yourself, Jack. Thank God now, and let later come
   later.
Lewis Anyway, it's not such a big miracle, really. You coming back to life.
Joy What's wrong with it? You leave my miracle alone.
Lewis You were alive before. I wasn't.
Joy What are you talking about?
Lewis I started living when I started loving you, Joy. That makes me only a
   few months old.
Joy Could be a short life, Jack.
Lewis At least it's a life.

*The screen rises to reveal the study at The Kilns. A third chair has been placed
there*

Joy and Lewis enter the study

   Welcome home!
Joy Let me do it myself. (*She hobbles into the room*) Jack, I have a question
   I've never dared ask before. But now that we're married . . .
Lewis Anything, Joy.
Joy Do you ever turn the central heating on?
Lewis I'm afraid it's broken.
Joy When did it stop working?
Lewis Good heavens, I can't remember. Ten years ago? Keep your coat on, I
   always do.

Joy This world is not a perfect place, Jack. And your house is less perfect than most of it. Will you let me purge it a little?
Lewis It's your home now, Joy. Purge away.

Joy hits a chair with her stick. Dust rises

Joy Look at that. (*She turns to him and strokes his shoulders*) And how about you? I'm not caressing you lovingly, I'm removing the dust. Actually I am caressing you lovingly.

They look into each others eyes. Lewis leans forward and kisses her. He helps her to the third chair, brings a footstool for her legs and covers her legs with a blanket. He then brings her a crossword puzzle and a pen

Joy Such service! I should get ill more often.

Lewis exits with her suitcase and one of her sticks

Warnie enters, reading a newspaper, and settles down in his usual chair

Douglas enters, carrying a chess board, set up with chess pieces, which he puts down on a side table. He ponders the game and eventually makes a move

Warnie (*reading aloud from his newspaper*) "The Queen has announced that the Royal Family's surname will be changed to Mountbatten-Windsor".
Joy "Quintessence. Botanically expressed." Four. I didn't know the Queen had a surname.
Warnie Used to be something foreign. Then it became Windsor. Pith. (*He reads more from the newspaper*) "The new surname will not apply until Prince Charles has grandsons." How very strange.

Warnie makes a move in the chess game

Lewis has now entered and stands behind Douglas, watching the game

Douglas Oh no! I didn't see that! Can't I have my move again?
Lewis You don't need to. Look. Check. (*He shows Douglas his next move*)
Douglas Oh yes!
Joy Make him work it out for himself, Jack. It's the only way he'll learn.
Lewis Is that so, Joy? Maybe we should send him to the University of Hard Knocks. He could learn to say: I don't know much about art, but I call a spade a spade.
Joy I knew it! That Honest Jack act you pull in your radio talks, it's all a front. You're an intellectual snob.
Lewis Oh really? And am I a "highbrow", and a "smug academic"?
Joy I'm not insulting you, Jack. I'm criticizing you.
Lewis I see. Please enlighten me.
Joy The educational system in this country is prehistoric. The boys at Douglas's school talk about going to university like it was going to the moon.
Lewis How is that a criticism of me? I'd like as many boys to go to university as possible.

Joy I counted three buried assumptions there. You'd "like"—that's the language of mild preference, not active concern. You don't say: "I'd like as many boys to be saved from starvation as possible".

Lewis My language reflects——

Joy Wait, I haven't finished. Second buried assumption: "boys". What about the girls?

Lewis Conceded. Go on.

Joy Third buried assumption: you'd like as many to go to university "as possible". What makes it possible, Jack? God? Chance? The weather? How about people like you? The high priests of the sacred cult of the intellectual élite.

Lewis Verbal raspberries.

Joy You always want the last word.

Lewis Precious hope of that.

Warnie speaks from behind his newspaper, surprising them both out of their argument

Warnie I've got it. Honeymoon.

Joy What?

Lewis What was that, Warnie?

Warnie Marriage. Honeymoon. That's the way of it. You should have a honeymoon.

Lewis Joy's not up to travelling.

Joy I suppose this is our honeymoon, Warnie.

Lewis I suppose it is.

Joy So how come we're carrying on as if we've been married for years?

Lewis Is that what we're doing?

Joy You are an intellectual bully, you know.

Lewis That makes two of us. I think I'm too old to change now. Do you mind?

Joy You being too old or you being a bully?

Lewis Either.

Joy No, I don't mind. Do you?

Lewis No. I don't want to be young any more. When you're young, you're always looking ahead, always waiting for something better to come round the next bend in the road. I'm not looking ahead any more. I'm with you, here, now, and that's enough.

Joy People go on journeys for their honeymoon, Jack.

Lewis What, you mean abroad?

Joy No need to sound so alarmed.

Lewis My mother took Warnie and me to Berneval, near Dieppe, the summer before she died. My one and only holiday abroad.

Warnie Nineteen hundred and seven.

Lewis Where do you want to go?

Joy I've always wanted to go to Greece. To see the Parthenon. And the temple of Apollo at Delphi. And the lion gates at Mycenae.

Lewis Where would we stay?

Joy Some little Greek hotel.

Lewis Are you up to it?

Joy Me? If you are.

Lewis I truly believe that if I had to go into an hotel with a woman, and sign the register, I'd blush.

Warnie That's settled then.

Joy "The Isles of Greece. The Isles of Greece."

As Joy and Lewis move DS *the screen falls behind them*

Joy
Lewis } *(together)* "Where burning Sappho loved and sung
Where grew the arts of war and peace
Where Delos rose and Phoebus sprung!
Eternal summer gilds them yet
But all except their sun is set."

Joy And there it is as advertised, not yet set. I love the sun. Don't you love the sun?

Lewis Dreadful glare, isn't there?

A waiter enters with their luggage

I never feel at ease in hotels. There's always someone hanging around trying to be helpful.

Joy Well, I like them. And I especially like room service.

Lewis Room service? I always used to believe that room service was saying prayers in bed.

Joy Well, you order some prayers if you want. Me, I want a gin and tonic.

Lewis Now? You only just had breakfast.

Joy So?

Lewis *(to the waiter)* All right. I'd like to order some drinks if we may, to be brought up to our room, if that's convenient. We'd like a gin and tonic, and a gin and tonic. So that's two gin and tonics . . . actually, two gins and tonic, to be strictly accurate.

The waiter exits

Joy You don't drink gin.

Lewis Yes, I know. I'm afraid I panicked.

Joy I love the sun. People used to worship the sun. I can understand it.

Lewis I can understand people who worship the sun in England where the sun is invisible, but here. Look at it, hanging around like a waiter hoping for a tip. This has no class. No mystery.

Joy No, Jack. It's a feeling. You just don't know how to be in the sun.

Lewis What do you mean?

Joy Come here and I'll show you.

Lewis You know I don't like surprises.

Joy Come over here.

Lewis This isn't going to work.

Joy Now put that face of yours up here. Feel it on your face. The sun so close you could stick out your tongue and lick it. No words. No thoughts. Just the sun on your face. The sound of the wind in the olive trees, and the cicadas. In this land nothing is impossible. Nothing is forbidden. You could even take off your coat.

Lewis Oh, I say, steady on.

The waiter enters with the drinks

Lewis hands Joy a drink

Lewis You all right?

Joy I'm fine. I'm great.

Lewis hands the drinks back to the waiter, who exits

As the screen rises, Lewis and Joy turn and move US

I am so happy. I don't think I've ever been so happy in my life.

Lewis Nor I. Not since the day I was elected a Fellow of Magdalen.

Joy No, kidding! I didn't think there was any experience to beat that this side of paradise.

Lewis This is paradise for me. Now.

Joy Don't say that, Jack. Paradise lasts. It's beautiful here. Being with you is everything I want. But it's not going to last.

Lewis We don't need to think of that now. I don't want to spoil the time we have together.

Joy It doesn't spoil it. It makes it precious. The small things, the ordinary things. Each time you touch me, I feel it like a shock. Your nearness. Your reality. You. (*She looks at him, forcing him to face what is coming*) What will you do when I die?

Lewis I don't know.

Joy I want to be with you then, Jack. The only way I can do that is to talk to you about it now.

Lewis I shall manage. Don't worry about me.

Joy I think it can be better than that. Better than just managing. What I'm trying to say is, that pain, then, is part of this happiness, now. That's the deal.

Lewis We'll have no clocks. No calendars. No clocks.

Joy I know your footsteps. I can tell it's you, long before you reach the house. I know it's you coming up the road.

Lewis I never thought I could be so happy, so late in life. Every day when I come home, there you are.

Joy The first words you speak, I know what kind of a mood you're in. Just from the sound of your voice. Even if you don't speak, I still know, from the lines on your face. I watch you when you're working at your desk. I study you. I learn you.

Lewis Every day when I come home, there you are. I can't get used to that. Every day, it surprises me. There you are. It's the sheer availability of the happiness that takes my breath away. I reach out and there you are. I hold you in my arms. I kiss you. All I have to do is reach out, and there you are. You've made the world kind to me and I'm so grateful. Grateful for all the ordinary domestic pleasures.

Joy Grateful. Yes.

The pain now returns to Joy. She feels it, but tries not to show it

Lewis I think I love you too much, Joy. I can't bear to see you in pain.
Joy The pain doesn't matter. It keeps me quiet.
Lewis When it gets close you find out whether you believe it or not.
Joy Only shadows, Jack. That's what you always say. Real life hasn't begun
yet. You'd just better be right. (*She slips into an exhausted sleep*)

Douglas enters. He looks at Joy, but doesn't know how to speak to her

Lewis draws him away

*During the following Warnie brings a footstool and blanket for Joy, kisses her
and exits*

Lewis Ah. Douglas. Your mother's very sick, I'm afraid.
Douglas She's going to die, isn't she?

Lewis doesn't know how to respond

Lewis She is very sick.
Douglas Why?
Lewis I don't know.
Douglas Can't you do something?
Lewis I'm afraid not.
Douglas OK.

Douglas exits

*Lewis draws a chair up beside Joy and sits down. For a few moments, he watches
her. Then he drifts into a half-sleep, exhausted himself*

The Lights change slowly, to night-time

Joy opens her eyes. She is very weak

Joy Still here?

Lewis wakes

Lewis Still here.
Joy Go to bed. Get some sleep.
Lewis Soon.
Joy Jack. Has it been worth it?
Lewis Three years of happiness?
Joy Tell me you'll be all right.
Lewis I'll be all right.
Joy Can we talk about it?
Lewis We've never pretended with each other.
Joy No. Never pretended.
Lewis Are you afraid?
Joy Of dying?
Lewis Yes.
Joy I'm tired, Jack. I want to rest. I just don't want to leave you.
Lewis I don't want you to go.

Joy Too much pain.
Lewis I know.
Joy Other worlds, Jack. It has to be more than we can imagine. Even more than you can imagine.
Lewis Far more.
Joy I love your other worlds. That was how I first started to love you. Long before I met you.
Lewis Just stories, Joy.
Joy Good stories.
Lewis I don't know what to do, Joy. You'll have to tell me what to do.
Joy You have to let me go, Jack.
Lewis I'm not sure that I can.

A silence. Joy is in too much pain to speak. Then the thought of her son breaks through, bringing another sort of pain

Joy Douglas—will you take care of——
Lewis Of course I will, Joy.
Joy He pretends not to mind.
Lewis I know.
Joy Like you.
Lewis No pretending any more.
Joy I've loved you so much, Jack.

Lewis takes her hand and presses it to his lips, trying not to show his own pain

It's always easier for the one who goes first.

He can see that the effort of talking is too much for her

Lewis Don't talk any more. You rest.

She nods her head and closes her eyes. By now all we can see are the two of them, deep in the night. Lewis sits with his chin resting in his hands, speaking softly into the darkness

Not much more to say. I love you, Joy. I love you so much. You've made me so happy. I didn't know I could be so happy. You're the truest person I've ever known. Sweet Jesus, be with my beloved wife, Joy. Forgive me if I love her too much. Have mercy on us both.

Joy's eyes open

Joy (*very faintly*) Go to bed, Jack. Get some sleep.
Lewis How's the pain?
Joy Not too good.
Lewis Only shadows, Joy.
Joy Only shadows. (*Her eyes close again*)

Lewis rises, stoops and kisses her, and walks softly out of the pool of light on Joy which fades slowly to Black-out as the screen comes in

The Lights come up again on Harrington, Gregg, and Riley

Harrington Naturally I wouldn't say this to Jack, but better sooner than later. Better quick than slow. After all, there was no question about it. The writing was on the wall.

Gregg Is he taking it very hard?

Harrington He's a remarkable man, Jack. Faith solid as a rock.

Riley Harry, those few well-chosen words at the church. Did I hear you correctly? It seemed to me you said something like "All who knew her loved her".

Harrington Something like that.

Riley Not quite God's own truth, was it?

Harrington Good grief, Christopher, what was I supposed to say? That nobody could stand her?

Riley Jack loved her. That's what's true, and that's what matters. But I didn't and you didn't.

Harrington But she's dead.

Riley Death does not improve the character.

The screen goes up and they join Warnie, who is seated at the college high table

Gregg You don't love anyone, Christopher, as far as I can see.

Riley That may well be true, but Harry still shouldn't tell whoppers.

Harrington Jack was standing six feet away.

Riley Jack wouldn't have minded. He's changed. She did that. She was a remarkable woman. But I'm damned if I'm going to start liking her just because she's dead.

Harrington Did you like her, Warnie?

Warnie Not at first. But oh, yes.

Lewis enters

An awkward silence falls as he comes to his place at table

Lewis I wasn't going to come. Then I thought I would. (*He sits. He sounds perfectly calm*)

Harrington Life must go on.

Lewis I don't know that it must. But it certainly does.

Gregg I'm sorry I wasn't able to be at the church.

Lewis Not important, Alan.

Harrington My little address, Jack. Was it . . . ?

Lewis Please forgive me, Harry. I haven't the slightest idea what you said in church. I didn't hear a word.

Harrington Fine. Fine. Perfectly understandable.

Riley Are you all right, Jack?

Lewis No.

Harrington Thank God for your faith, Jack. Where would you be without that?

Lewis I'd be here, drinking my port.

Harrington What I mean to say, Jack, is that it's only faith that makes any sense of times like this.

Lewis puts down his glass

Lewis I'm sorry, Harry, but it won't do. This is a mess, and that's all there is to it.

Harrington A mess?

Lewis What sense do you make of it? You tell me.

Harrington But, Jack—we have to have faith that God knows——

Lewis God knows. Yes, God knows. I don't doubt that. God knows. But does God care? Did he care about Joy?

Harrington Why are you talking like this, Jack? We can't see what's best for us. You know that. We're not the Creator.

Lewis No. We're the creatures. We're the rats in the cosmic laboratory. I've no doubt the great experiment is for our own good, eventually, but that still makes God the vivisectionist.

Harrington This is your grief talking.

Lewis What was talking before? My complacency?

Harrington Please, Jack. Please.

Lewis I'm sorry, Harry. You're a good man. I don't mean to distress you. But the fact is, I've come up against a bit of experience recently. Experience is a brutal teacher, but you learn fast. I'm sorry. I shouldn't have come this evening. I'm not fit company. (*He rises*) If you'll forgive me. (*He leaves the table*)

Warnie Excuse me.

Warnie follows his brother to where he stands downstage, frowning, by himself. The screen falls

> *The others exit when the screen is in place*

Lewis Sorry about that, Warnie. Not necessary.

Warnie Everybody understands, Jack.

Lewis I can't see her any more. I can't remember her face. What's happening to me?

Warnie I expect it's shock.

Lewis I'm so terribly afraid. Of never seeing her again. Of thinking that suffering is just suffering after all. No cause. No purpose. No pattern. No sense. Just pain, in a world of pain.

Warnie I don't know what to tell you, Jack.

Lewis Nothing. There's nothing to say.

They are silent for a few moments

> *Douglas enters on the far side of the stage. He is profoundly hurt by his mother's death, but is refusing to show it*

Warnie Jack.

Lewis Yes.

Warnie About Douglas.

Lewis Yes.

Warnie Your grief is your business. Maybe you feel life is a mess. Maybe it is. But he's only a child.

Lewis What am I supposed to do about it?

Warnie Talk to him.

Lewis I don't know what to say to him.
Warnie Just talk to him.

Warnie exits

Lewis walks slowly across to Douglas. He speaks to the boy in a matter-of-fact way; as if they are equals

Lewis When I was your age, my mother died. That was cancer too. I thought that if I prayed for her to get better, and if I really believed she'd get better, then she wouldn't die. But she did.
Douglas It doesn't work.
Lewis No. It doesn't work.
Douglas I don't care.
Lewis I do. When I'm alone, I start crying. Do you cry?
Douglas No.
Lewis I didn't when I was your age.

A brief pause

I loved your mother very much.
Douglas That's OK.
Lewis I loved her too much. She knew that. She said to me, "Is it worth it?" She knew how it would be later. It doesn't seem fair, does it? If you want the love, you have to have the pain.
Douglas I don't see why she had to get sick.
Lewis Nor me.

Another pause

You can't hold on to things. You have to let them go.
Douglas Jack?
Lewis Yes.
Douglas Do you believe in heaven?
Lewis Yes.
Douglas I don't believe in heaven.
Lewis That's OK.
Douglas I sure would like to see her again.
Lewis Me too.

Douglas can't take any more. He reaches out for comfort, pressing himself against Lewis. Lewis wraps his arms round the boy, and at last his own tears break through, in heart-breaking sobs, unloosing the grief of a lifetime. His emotion releases the tears that have been waiting in the boy

As they fall quiet, Douglas detaches himself, and exits

Lewis turns to face the audience, and begins to speak quietly. His words are a version of the talk he has given earlier, now transformed by his own suffering

We are like blocks of stone, out of which the sculptor carves the forms of men. The blows of his chisel, which hurt us so much, are what makes us perfect.

No shadows here. Only darkness, and silence, and the pain that cries like a child.

It ends, like all affairs of the heart, with exhaustion. Only so much pain is possible. Then, rest.

So it comes about that, when I am quiet, when I am quiet, she returns to me. There she is, in my mind, in my memory, coming towards me and I love her again as I did before, even though I know I will lose her again, and be hurt again.

So you can say if you like that Jack Lewis has no answer to the question after all, except this: I have been given the choice twice in my life. The boy chose safety. The man chooses suffering.

He now speaks to her, in his memory

I went to my wardrobe this morning. I was looking for my old brown jacket, the one I used to wear before—I'd forgotten that you'd carried out one of your purges there. Just before we went to Greece, I think it was.

I find I can live with the pain after all. The pain, now, is part of the happiness, then. That's the deal.

Only shadows, Joy.

CURTAIN

FURNITURE AND PROPERTY LIST

ACT I

On stage: Outer Area
Tree with magic apples
Books on bookshelves

Inner Area
Large high-table. *On it:* silver table settings, glasses, decanter of port, etc.
Beneath it: scarves and hats for **Warnie** and **Lewis**

Personal: **Lewis:** wrist-watch (worn throughout), newspaper
Warnie: wrist-watch (worn throughout)

When the screen in place (page 4)
Inner Area
Strike: High-table and six chairs
Set: Desk. *On it:* pens, papers, books, etc.
Chair
Armchair
Small table

Off stage: Bicycle **(Gregg)**
Tray of breakfast items, letters (including airmail letter), newspaper
(Warnie)

When screen in place (page 7)
Inner Area
Strike: Breakfast items, tray, newspaper, letters

Outer Area
Set: Tea table and four chairs DL. *On table:* bell

Off stage: Hardback edition of *The Magician's Nephew* **(Douglas)**
Tray of tea items **(Waiter)**

The screen rises (page 12)
Outer Area
Strike: Tea table and four chairs

Off stage: Paper chains **(Warnie)**
Tray of tea items, including glass of squash and cake **(Lewis)**
Glasses **(Warnie, Riley, Oakley** and **Harrington)**
Breakfast tray, newspaper **(Warnie)**
Letters **(Lewis)**
Typescript **(Riley)**

Personal: **Lewis:** money, fountain pen
Waiter: note-pad, pencil
Joy: airmail letter

When screen in place (page 23)
        Inner Area
Strike: All items
Set: Packing cases containing books and various items wrapped in newspaper
              Bookshelves

When screen in place (page 27)
        Inner Area
Strike: Items

Set: Table. *On it:* pen, register, service book

Off stage: Deckchair, book **(Warnie)**
             Deckchair, book **(Lewis)**
             Pile of books **(Lewis)**

When screen in place (page 29)
        Inner Area
Strike: All items

Set: Armchair and **Lewis's** coat

ACT II

            Outer Area
Set: Chair DR

            Inner Area
            Hospital bed with bedclothes and pillows
            Chair

Off stage: Book **(Douglas)**

When screen in place (page 35)
        Outer Area
Strike: Chair DR

Off stage: Service book **(Priest)**
             Hospital screens **(Nurse)**

Personal: **Warnie:** wedding ring in pocket

When screen in place (page 41)
        Inner Area
Set: Crutches and coat for **Joy**

Re-set: Hospital screens around bed

When screen in place (page 44)
        Inner Area
Strike: All items

Set: Desk. *On it:* pens, papers, books, etc.
              Chair
              Armchair
              Small table
              Chair

Off stage: Newspaper **(Warnie)**
          Chessboard and pieces **(Douglas)**

When screen in place (page 47)
          Inner Area
Strike: All items

Set: Sofa
          Telephone

During Black-out (page 50)
          Inner Area
Strike: All items

Set: High-table. *On it:* silver table settings, glasses, decanter of port, etc.
          Six chairs

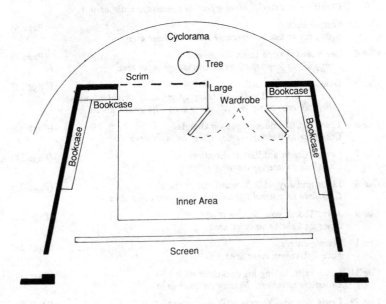

LIGHTING PLOT

Practical fittings required: glowing "magic apples"

Various interior and exterior settings

ACT I

To open: General on downstage outer area

ACT II

To open: General lighting on downstage outer area

EFFECTS PLOT

ACT I

Cue 1 **Lewis:** "'Strike the bell, and bide the danger.'" (Page 11)
Music

Cue 2 The screen rises (Page 12)
Wardrobe doors open slowly

Cue 3 **Douglas** enters the magic world (Page 12)
Wardrobe doors close slowly; fade music

Cue 4 **Warnie:** "'A distinctive voice.'" (Page 12)
Doorbell

Cue 5 **Lewis:** "I know." (Page 21)
Doorbell

Cue 6 Lewis takes up his chair and exits (Page 28)
Thunder

Cue 7 **Lewis, Joy** and **Warnie** walk downstage (Page 29)
Sound of rain

Cue 8 **Warnie** and **Joy** exit (Page 29)
Cut rain effect

ACT II

Cue 9 **Priest:** ". . . from this day forward." (Page 38)
Wardrobe doors open slowly

Cue 10 **Douglas** kisses his mother (Page 39)
Wardrobe doors close slowly

MADE AND PRINTED IN GREAT BRITAIN BY
LATIMER TREND & COMPANY LTD PLYMOUTH
MADE IN ENGLAND